Anna Gitszel

BLACKSHEEP

How to grow up in HELL and not become a DEVIL

D1619578

Written down by Anna Gajowniczek

Edition: Joanna Sosnowka
Translation: Limitless Mind Publishing
Proofreading: Maria Berdysz
Text Composition: InkWander
Cover Design: Malgorzata Sokolowska
Cover photo: Michael Eitenbenz

ISBN: 9788397031838

Limitless Mind Publishing Ltd
15 Carleton Road
Chichester
PO19 3NX
England
Tel. +44 7747761146
Email: office@limitlessmindpublishing.com

Dear Reader!

*Find us on **Facebook/Instagram:***
limitless mind publishing

*And visit our page on **Amazon***
by entering: limitless mind publishing into the search bar
or by scanning the QR code to see our other titles.

♥ We would greatly appreciate your opinion. It means a lot to us.

To every woman who, like me, had a tough time in her life.
And she did not give up.

I am proud of you.

Author's Note

You are going to read a story that left a mark on my soul and made me who I am today. The story of a girl, and then a woman who endured misery and became a happy and valuable person. They say that there are no failures in life, only lessons that you have prepared for yourself to learn how to live. Every story is different, and coming back to mine once again makes me feel incredibly relieved and grateful for what I have right now. Because our past, when we can understand it, does not have to determine who we are in the present.

So, you are going to read about a girl who was ten years old when her father hit her for the first time. A girl whom her brother introduced to the violent world of sex without consent only two years later. A fourteen-year-old who could not stand her dysfunctional family anymore and got involved with a man who was ten years older, so that he could get her away from the bleak reality. A girl who despite all that tried to kill herself only once, when she was fifteen. A woman who ended up dancing in German strip clubs.

You are also going to read about the indifference I witnessed which I still fail to understand. About how people are unable to step out of their comfort zone to help someone, maybe even save someone else's life. Nobody saw my father kicking me on the way home. Nobody heard me scream when he hit me again and again. Nobody saw my mother fleeing home after another row. Nobody intervened when my brother forced the door one more time. People usually turn a blind eye to the problems of others and it was one of those truths that I could not comprehend.

Such childhood instilled in my head many negative beliefs about life. As an adult, I chose a path that would compensate me for the past, yet I still could not let it go. That is why you are going to read about the transitional period in my life when I settled for dancing in strip clubs. This part of my life showed me that peace, health, and living in harmony with oneself are more important than money and designer clothes.

And luckily for me, the Universe guided me to where I am today. Because remember, it always works in your favor. You just have to let it be on your side.

Writing about my childhood, I often turned my thoughts to my adult life. It has been and still is a form of autotherapy. I always knew that even the worst situation would end. When I was being hurt I swore to myself with clenched teeth that someday I would retaliate. But this book is not a revenge. Thanks to the methods I got to know during my personal/spiritual growth I no longer seek revenge. Although the memories are still painful, I feel that only loving myself and forgiving my tormentors will help me to continue going through life in peace and harmony.

The proper names of most of the places described and names outside my family have been changed.

HELL

MY CHILDHOOD AND MY FAMILY

Introduction

Today, I cannot with full certainty determine the sequence of all the situations in which my father hit me. There were so many that they blended, often merging into one painful continuum. However, I will try to describe everything I felt back then and give shape to these situations, to better convey the hell I had to live in. I've retained the essence, and that's enough to step into my world if only a little.

I will never forget the moments when I ran to the stairwell to feel a bit safer. Sometimes I slept there. I often hid there from my brother. Fortunately, I could also hide at my friends' houses, which I did much more frequently. I won't forget the taste of my first drugs and alcohol, which I also sought as an escape. And I won't forget the pain I felt as I slowly lost trust in others and lost touch with myself. But I also won't forget the moment when I decided to never let anyone hit me again or cause me pain in any form. The moment I began to regain control over my life.

Many people after the age of thirty might have similar childhood experiences. Moreover, their parents probably see nothing wrong with their actions. Mine genuinely don't when it comes to what happened when we were children, and for me as a mother, it's incomprehensible. The child-rearing pattern of those times was as hurtful as it could be. "Dysfunction" is a very mild term for considering belts and beating to be methods of upbringing, not something that could harm. Violating other people's boundaries, a lack of intimacy in daily life, and the need to behave only according to the rules set by the limited imagination of society are particularly harmful. How was it that some families still managed to provide their children with security, love, and stable emotional support? Perhaps the parents of these children were guided by closeness, intuition, and simply an awareness that a child feels that they are a separate human being, and a parent should guide them through the world with empathy, not the compulsion of fulfilling their own vision. Unfortunately, that era did not favor such a pattern, and although there were loving families, many also suffered greatly.

The lack of emotional connection with parents hurts deeply. When a child is young, they still love unconditionally, and they internalize everything that happens around them. Thoughts often converge into one powerful emotion, signaling the child's perceived lack of worth. A child doesn't stop loving their parents just like that; it's a process. Perhaps a damaged love for the parents always remains within them. What the child primarily loses, however, is self-love. Instead, they start to believe they don't deserve attention, and a lack of conversation, tenderness, and support becomes their daily reality. Is it truly worth showing a child that the world is such a difficult, painful, and hostile place for them?

Anna

When it turns out that fear doesn't want to leave

As we begin to see the light at the end of the tunnel, we may find that there's work to be done in areas we weren't previously aware of. Issues related to physical abuse, violation of personal boundaries, or verbal aggression are evident, but there are also other emotional wounds that need attention. Therapy can be immensely helpful in this matter, but often, an everyday or random situation can also point the way. That's why it's worth being observant and paying attention to the slightest emotional tremors that may be a subtle hint of the unseen work ahead.

At one point in my therapy, I realized that the fear rooted in my childhood was still holding onto me tightly. A situation I discussed with my therapist made me aware of this. From my house, one gets outdoors via a set of stairs. We have a small backyard with a playground for children, which in turn leads directly to the street. I was sitting on the bed with a phone in my hand and for a mere few seconds lost sight of my younger, eighteen-month-old son. In that brief time, he went down those stairs. When I looked up, he was gone. Fear made me practically leap down the fifteen steps, and I found him just before he reached the street. One could argue it's a common situation, but what matters here is that the emotions from it lingered with me for weeks. Another instance was when my partner was driving and made a turn a bit too fast while our young one was in the front seat. Nothing happened, but the fear didn't let me let them go anywhere alone for the next three months.

Eventually, I grasped why this panic surfaces and why this fear is so strong, holding such immense power over me. It stems from the fact that my entire childhood was overshadowed by fear. Such a reaction is natural for my body because, over all those years, it became conditioned to this particular pattern. What's most crucial is that I'm aware of this and consciously notice such situations. By allowing myself to feel and accept the fear, I can let it go. Over time, it will weaken, remaining only as a faint qualm.

More than twenty-five years have passed since some events, yet I still live with the fear that clung to me then. Everyone scared me. Everything did. My imagination operated entirely out of control, always pulling me toward panic whenever I encountered a potentially dangerous situation.

I also recalled something that breaks my heart today, as a mother. When I was a little girl, around four or five years old, I was often left home alone. Each time, I'd hide behind the bed and could sit there until someone from the household returned. I remember how terrified I was then. How much tension must I have unknowingly nurtured within myself? I also recall the dread I felt when I had to go down to the basement for potatoes. It's indescribable how unsettling that place and moment were for me. I can't say why. I never went about it thinking of fetching potatoes as a mere household chore. But these are just some of the situations that were part of my daily life at that time.

I was afraid of the dark because other kids scared me with tales of two-headed monsters, and for any slight reason, my parents would lock me in the apartment storage room, which was both cramped and dark.

In a family album later in life, I found a photo of me sleeping on the floor of that storage room. My parents locked me in a small, dark space in the apartment, but I tried to suppress that memory. I can recall some fragments of this happening, yet everything is hazy. However, that photo is evidence to me that these are not just my dreams.

I feared the forest because I heard from adults that a rapist or a dangerous bull awaited me there. All this still haunts me. Loneliness brings me anxiety, and for a long time, I couldn't even board a train alone. I was afraid of relationships because my father told me that men would only be with me to exploit me. I remember him warning me about everyone, as in his opinion, everything around was evil; every man wanted to harm me. I was scared of heights. I was afraid to leave this life for the unknown because, although my surroundings were deeply hurtful, they were still familiar.

For many, many years, I was afraid of my father. I feared my brother. My grandmother. I was scared to go to school and scared to stay home. I was afraid to speak up, but I also feared the silence. Eventually, I became afraid to get out of bed, fearing punishment for another thing I couldn't comprehend. At some point, fear consumed my entire life. And in my teenage years, I believed in the only version of my future I knew then, the one my father painted for me: that I'd amount to nothing. That I'd spiral downward. Become homeless. Unworthy of a glance. Of tenderness.

That it was time for me to disappear because my life was meaningless.

In adulthood, many situations still can make my heart race. For a long time, I couldn't sleep without a light on, feeling I wasn't alone. Just taking a shower in the home bathroom would cause my cortisol levels to spike at an incredible rate, as memories of my brother peeping at me from the grate at the bottom of the shower door flooded back. I was long afraid of swimming because my mother once nearly drowned. I also hesitated to get a driver's license, due to the same fear. That very fear resurfaced at the thought of having a second child. Slowly, this fear is leaving me, but the realization that my life up to this point was dictated solely by it, is both melancholy and painfully profound.

Today, I know I am a wonderful mother with two amazing children. Both are incredibly intelligent and fearless. And I support and encourage them in their small and big challenges, ensuring that they always know they can achieve anything.

When I came into this world

I didn't ask to be born, and I don't think I intended to be a part of a family that didn't want me. This was supposed to be my first lesson. The first few days after birth are moments of great wisdom for a child, but subdued by mundane daily life, this wisdom gradually fades, eventually being replaced by what the surrounding environment imposes. And later, to reclaim that wisdom, one must know how.

I was the second child, the second one by chance. From what I found out many years later, I was also not necessarily desired. After giving birth to me, my mother had to live a life she didn't want. Her frustration seeped into my core, teaching me that life was a string of misfortunes, failures, and pain. From the stories, I know that before we came into the world, she worked in a pharmaceutical factory where she was soon to be promoted. She loved that job.

She yearned for growth; she wanted to pursue studies and travel. I can only guess that because of us, her children, she had to set aside her dreams for tasks she couldn't bear. Perhaps she never truly realized how much we craved her support and, at least once, a true display of love.

I was an honest, joyful toddler, especially in those earliest years. I recall moments when I felt genuinely good—brief instances that let me believe that, at least for a moment, I was a regular child, content with life. I had bright, short, curly hair that danced upon my head with every movement. I loved colorful clothes, rejoiced in play, and treasured days when I could feel safe.

I vividly remember times when life felt thrilling, moments when energy surged through me, hinting at something that could transform my life for the better. In the first few years of my life, I was filled with unbridled joy—a sentiment evident even in some of my childhood photos. A little girl who wanted to, and did, experience moments of peace, had hope for the future, and could live in the present. I remember this time as a somewhat blurry image. Perhaps it was during that phase that my parents gave me something akin to safety or at least its semblance. But back then, I didn't seem like a distinct entity. I was the sweet child of my parents, always underfoot. Do I remember love? I'm not sure, and that in itself speaks volumes.

Supposedly, my father rejoiced when I was born. He supposedly wanted me! Allegedly he loved me, and when he held me for the first time, he began pouring out a love that later turned out to be conditional. I was the apple of his eye, his beloved daughter, the light in his days after grueling work at the steel mill. I was an anchor for a man battered by life, who, just like my mother, turned out to be emotionally immature. Unfortunately, he failed to realize that true love is unconditional. When I no longer met his expectations, it all ended. Maybe I would have remembered that initial time on earth fondly. Maybe I would have recalled more if I hadn't experienced the disappointment of being relegated to the status of a stubborn, disobedient child.

When life passes you by

In theory, where we live shouldn't affect us. Of course, I'm referring to places that meet all our basic needs: shelter, warmth, clothes, food. But the same is provided to orphaned children who end up in foster homes. So can a child with a complete family suffer? Can they feel a void, even though, theoretically, they have what's needed to survive?

It's essential to note the stark difference between living and merely surviving. One can have the means to keep the body functioning at a basic level and yet feel nothing that allows them to enjoy interacting with the world. The same applies to one's living conditions. You can have the basics for life; you can even have everything and more in material terms and still feel empty inside. On the other hand, an entire family might live in a studio apartment and feel incredibly happy. But yes, you'd need to have a family, not just individuals responsible for bringing you into the world.

Honestly, it would be hard for me to call the place I grew up in "home." I spent my entire childhood in one location, had a roof over my head, and enough to eat. An outsider might conclude that I had no real reason to complain. But what good were those four walls if the only warmth I felt came from the radiators? A child growing up alone, among various individuals, won't develop a proper worldview. I can be thankful for the mere fact of being born and reaching this point in my life. Perhaps all of it had a deeper purpose, but my memories won't disappear; I can only frame them differently to free myself from them.

My childhood home was an apartment in a block, much like any other, maybe even a bit larger than most. I still have a clear image of it in my mind, and as an adult, I frequently visited my father's mother there, so I believe it's not something I'll ever completely forget. Upon entering the medium-sized hallway, you could freely move to the other rooms. To the left of the entrance were the doors to a reasonably sized bathroom. Those doors, in particular, seemed to offer me a false sense of security, but I'll delve into that later. A bit further, slightly to the left and opposite the entrance, was the door to a small room that my brother and I shared. I remember things were constantly being moved around there. The fairly large windows that overlooked the playground gave an illusion of more space than there was. Eventually, that room had to accommodate our younger sister, which meant there was hardly any space left, let alone any privacy as we reached our teenage years.

To the right of our room was a long, narrow kitchen. Under the window was a table, and along the wall were all the essential cooking utensils. It's hard for me to say if it was comfortable, as that reality was the only one I knew then. So, I never contemplated if a different room would have been a more suitable kitchen. Further to the right was the entrance to a large room, which served as the living room and our parents' bedroom. From there, you could access a spacious balcony, which I managed to escape to a few times when fleeing from my brother.

From one perspective, my upbringing didn't seem to differ from that of many children my age. But I can say with certainty that those walls and furnishings evoke no warmth or nostalgia for me. Based on all my childhood memories, it's more a place of sorrow and unexpressed regret.

I was allowed to be a child there only momentarily before being brutally thrust into adapting to the perceptions and actions of my loved ones. Every room could have been filled with joyous memories, but it represents the exact opposite. Nearly every item in that apartment might stir unpleasant recollections of my past.

When You Mistake Abusers for Friends

It is said that parents remain a child's favorite people only until about the age of ten. After that, a child or a young teenager shifts their affection to peers. But what if parents have always been, and continue to be, unavailable? What if the company a child keeps with pollutes their mind, destroying the last vestiges of self-love? The child then settles for crumbs and accepts the world as it's presented to them. It becomes natural for them not to know love, support, respect, and the value of oneself.

In my group, there were Karolina, Klaudia, Martyna, and Iza, Karolina's younger sister. I remember we began hanging out when I was around thirteen.

Karolina was the oldest and by far the most dangerous. She used drugs, got into fights, and intimidated others. The beginning of our friendship seemed alright, but tensions that mirrored those I experienced at home began to emerge, making it hard for me to cut ties. After school, we'd drink or smoke, and on one occasion after such a meet-up, she assaulted me. I didn't know how to defend myself, so she continued unhindered, with no retaliation from me. She just hit me. She pulled my hair, split my lips, and blackened my eyes.

Martyna was Karolina's cousin. Her childhood was far from idyllic. Her father had abandoned her before she was born. She lived with her mother and younger sister in subsidized housing, where she occasionally met with Karolina. Her later relationship with her father was incredibly complicated. He lived in the same town but always treated her like she was invisible. After many years, they reconnected, but their relationship was far from ideal. Martyna, like the rest of us, had a strong inclination for alcohol, drugs, and violence.

Klaudia was the least aggressive, but her family was shady. Her father had been in prison for many years. Her mom also went to jail, only later, for murder. Her brother landed in juvie. The only thing that made me different from them was living on a better estate and the fact that my parents had a car.

In our homes, a similar narrative played out. Pathological behavior, aggression, neglect, alcohol, and a complete lack of understanding. Not to mention the absence of love. In this group, I assumed the role of the victim. Karolina and Martyna took out their physical and emotional frustrations on me, while Klaudia somewhat stood on the sidelines. We often skipped school together and hitchhiked. But almost every trip ended the same way, with me being beaten up.

All this came to an end when I left, but a pivotal moment for me, after about four years of our acquaintance, was when I fell in love. I was seventeen then. We were at a party in a neighboring city at another friend's place. Marcin was there, someone I had a crush on and I felt that he reciprocated my feelings. We drank, and at some point, everyone fell asleep. I lay beside Marcin, and Karolina lay down at his other side. I woke up to them having sex. Marcin was so drunk he didn't even realize who he was with. Time seemed to freeze as I watched, realizing just how far Karolina would go to humiliate me at every turn.

When I lifted my head and Marcin realized he wasn't sharing this less-than-intimate moment with me, he stopped immediately. He profusely apologized, clearly disoriented. He didn't know what to do, and I didn't know what to say. I was shell-shocked, but it made me understand that there was nothing Karolina wouldn't do to hurt me.

An hour after that incident, he left. He apologized numerous times later, but it meant nothing to me because I couldn't comprehend it. This incident tainted my trust in other men I got involved with. Until the age of twenty-six, control was like a compulsion. When partners went to shower, I would go through their phones, checking everything, feeling myself burning inside. But eventually, I realized the futility of it all. If someone intends to betray me, they will. Trust is foundational, and I cannot control everything around me.

Our relationships shape our character, and when we neither have friends around us nor a friend within us, it's challenging to lead a happy and fulfilling life.

Zbigniew

When a Man Becomes a Father

A father should be a figure of authority, a pillar of support for his family, and someone to whom one can always turn for advice. He also serves as a model of manhood for his daughter, who, especially in her early years, often idolizes him without question. A strong and positive relationship with a father empowers a girl to grow into a confident woman with a robust sense of self-worth. How a father treats the mother, how he spends time with her and their children, the way he narrates the world, and the words he uses daily lay the foundation for a child's development.

However, my father was primarily my tormentor—a man who disappointed me in every aspect of life. Born into a dysfunctional family, his parents failed to instill any positive values in him. His emotionless and unempathetic mother, coupled with a father subservient to her whims, was incapable of raising a child to be happy and emotionally stable. From a young age, my father was made to feel superior to others, though without any real basis for such an attitude. My paternal grandmother pretended to be exceedingly wealthy, even though in her daily life she scrimped on necessities like water for basic baths. Living in the countryside, she always gave off the impression that money was no object for her. Yet, she concealed not just their actual emotional and financial poverty but also her husband's issues, either failing to recognize them or fiercely defending them due to her sense of superiority. It was in this environment that my father must have felt victimized, growing up in a physical sense but trapped in the mindset of a perpetually demanding and expectant child.

When I was a few years old, he quit his job at the steel mill to work abroad, taking up employment in Germany. He would return to us every few months, perhaps for two weeks at a time. During these visits, he would subject us to physical abuse, humiliation, and degradation, shattering the fragile equilibrium we'd managed to establish in his absence. Was he unleashing the bitterness of his life onto us? Some internal pain? Resentment that we weren't perfect? I don't know, and frankly, I don't want to know. When I was born, he was young but mature enough. He should have then taken responsibility for me and my siblings and tackled his unresolved issues, rather than deflecting and justifying his behavior by saying he was bringing money home. Each time he left again, we needed days to lick our wounds and heal. We were denied the right to grow in self-love.

One night, I was awakened by my father's shouts as my mother, clad only in her robe, tried to flee our house. She hesitated for a moment at the door, and that's when my father yanked her back inside.

"Be quiet" he hissed menacingly, all the while striking her across the face.

"Why wake the children...?" I could hear her sobbing, but the venomous words spat out by my father were louder and clearer:

"The next time you do this, I'll kill you. Understand?"

After hearing that, I was petrified to get up, but I knew I had to at some point. I couldn't reconcile that my dad, the same one who'd take me out for ice cream and playfully hoist me onto his shoulders, could utter such threats. He hadn't hit me yet; I was about seven or eight years old, and I couldn't fathom why he would hit her. It deeply affected me, and I avoided speaking to him. Of course, he acted as if nothing had happened. Later, I learned that the reason he beat my mother that night was because she had lent someone money. So, my father punished her for helping someone. From a very young age, fear was an integral part of my relationship with him. When he eventually started hitting me, it seemed like a perverse confirmation of my worst fears. I remember feeling utterly shattered that night.

That fear still grips me every time I think back to it.

When I Started to Fade Away

For a child, naturally exploring the world is essential for growth. Learning the right reactions, having the ability to express oneself, and receiving responses are foundational at every developmental stage. If someone inhibits a child's behavior and proper growth simply because it doesn't align with their perceptions, they inflict enormous harm on the child, disrupting their essence.

The moment I received that first slap, meant to brutally put my thoughts and opinions in their place, I felt fear. Yet, along with that fear came a belief: it was my father who was undeserving of respect, not me. From that point on, I held my tongue around him, and what appeared to be a happy childhood simply ended. Adulthood felt a long way off, signifying that I had fallen into a void where I'd remain for many more years.

My bond with my father vanished entirely. In his presence, I felt restless and threatened. He became my tormentor, reinforcing my belief that he was unfit to be a father. His views on parenting and raising a child were detached from reality if he had any views at all. I became his disappointment, and the mere act of my speaking became a bone of contention. But soon, other things, too, drove him to fits of rage. Shortly after the initial hit, I received a lifelong memento. I vividly recall the betrayal, the lack of understanding, and the pain – not just physical. When this supposedly grown man lashed my back with a thick leather belt, I could swear he wasn't thinking. A new friend of my mother's accused me of stealing her gold bracelet. He didn't even ask for my side of the story, just acted on the accusation, leaving three long scars on my back. I couldn't fathom why he wouldn't listen, why he'd believe someone living in a social housing unit without a single piece of furniture and two kids to support. And with a possibly not-so-innocent lover behind bars. The shock and feeling of the rug being pulled from under me led me to ask God to take me away for the first time. Given His silence, I withdrew into myself, sinking deeper into darkness.

Once he started, he'd hit me for truancy and alleged thefts. Eventually, he'd hit me for anything. I remember he even struck me because a friend's boyfriend, perhaps Marcel, called me. The exchange was short and aggressive. First, my father was upset that anyone called me at all, then, likely in response to some backtalk, threatened the guy that another call might end very badly for him. I listened to the conversation, book in hand. When he hung up, he approached me and struck me so hard across the face that the book fell from my grasp.

Was it my fault? That someone called me? That he would get upset over it? Should violence truly be the first, or any, response to such a thing? I was utterly bewildered. Now, would I also be punished for other people's actions?

To this day, I can't understand how an adult can treat their child like that. Especially since I have my kids now and could never do to them what has been deeply imprinted on my memory. His role in my life had been significant, dragging me down for many years. He's just the man who brought me into this world; I can't recall any other positive memories related to him. He took everything from me, completely disregarding my needs.

Nowadays, in many situations, teachers, neighbors, or even strangers can intervene when they see a child slowly becoming a shadow of themselves, showing signs of abuse, having trust issues, or cutting off deeper relationships. Of course, it's not always the case, but back then, I was completely alone. If anyone suspected what was truly happening, they turned away, not wanting to pollute their world with someone else's problems, even if it could save my life.

I remember being jealous of my friends because they had safe homes. One of them was Ola, who lived in a single-family house nearby. Her parents occasionally picked her up from school and took her out for walks, dinners, or anything else that would allow them to spend quality time together. She always wore clean, neat clothes, and her school supplies were always complete. She often told me stories about what she did with her parents after school. Her mom would surprise her after tests, regardless of the grades she got. She also talked about how her mom would help her with homework and genuinely participate in her daily life, supporting her in everything she did. All of this was natural for her, while I was scared to step into the apartment I lived in. She could talk, hug, and tell her parents about her day. Meanwhile, I spent those same tension-filled days waiting for the moment when I would be punished for being myself, or rather, for what I allegedly did. The only time I felt relatively safe was when my father was at work. Those days were brighter for me, and coming home wasn't so scary. Sadly, this didn't last long, as my trust in people eventually disappeared.

My neighborhood was a gathering place for many kids. I remember moments when I could join their games, but also times when I had to abstain. I recall the conversations and laughter that I would hear through my open apartment window as I lay inside, crying after yet another severe beating. I can't even begin to count the many minutes, hours, and months of my life I lost, healing my bruised body, soothing aching muscles, or escaping into sleep to avoid reality. The numbing pain started making me feel like I deserved all of this, that what was happening to me was somehow normal. Of course, I rebelled at times, sometimes more, sometimes less, but the frequency of these incidents was alarming, especially since I was just a child.

So many times, I found myself wishing for death, no longer even wanting love from my father, whose touch only caused me pain.

When there's no way out

Not always do we want to talk, and avoiding difficult topics is a daily routine, especially during heightened stress, fatigue, or an overload of unre-

lated thoughts. Escaping into silence helps to soothe the mind and gives us a chance to constructively address a situation. The right reaction when someone doesn't want to discuss something is to let it go, not harass or force them to answer. Unfortunately, not everyone can handle this, and some tend to push others into uncomfortable conversations when they're truly not up to it. While a healthy adult can deal with an awkward question or situation, an undeveloped mind reacts entirely differently. When a child doesn't respond to a question, looks away, and pretends not to hear, they're avoiding confrontation. For some reason, they don't feel safe or comfortable enough to answer.

Until I was seventeen, I lived in my family's apartment because I didn't know any other way. Weekends, I remember, were another nightmare for me. It seemed I always had a plan. I wouldn't get up for breakfast; after waking up, I'd lie in bed for several more hours, pretending to sleep. I feared that the moment I rose, my father would find another reason to hit me. I would only get up when he came to wake me. Then, I'd go to the shower, sitting there as long as I possibly could. But eventually, I had to face reality and come out to start the day. Typically, the whole family would visit relatives, and then spend time having lunch and engage in never-ending, aimless conversations. These trips were both a relief and another source of stress for me. I prayed they'd last as long as possible, constantly checking the clock. The longer we stayed with family or friends, the higher the chances that my father would be too tired to lay a hand on me after returning home. But it was always a gamble.

One day, during yet another weekend, my father took my brother and me to a friend's house to help him fix his car. We were supposed to stay in our car, sit quietly, and wait patiently. I was hoping for several hours of peace, but around 4 p.m., I saw him coming back to us. When he got into the car, he had a smile on his face.

"I want to tell you both something important," he said, still smiling. We stayed silent, prompting him to continue.

"I've thought about everything, and I want to start fresh. I won't hit you anymore. Just stop causing trouble and don't do things that would embarrass me. How does that sound?"

"Okay!" I blurted out, feeling a genuine surge of happiness. I truly believed that this nightmare was over and that I wouldn't be hit again. However, I couldn't understand what he meant by not doing things that would make him feel embarrassed. It felt like immense pressure. There were moments, especially in public, where I was terrified to even make a move, fearing it might upset him. I remember times when I'd sit at a table for half an hour, pondering whether it'd be okay for me to get up and use the restroom.

We returned home that day in a lighter atmosphere than usual. But it didn't take long to realize that my father's promise would not be kept. Perhaps he momentarily felt the urge to overcome the disappointment he saw in me, or maybe he genuinely believed things would change. Unfortunately, that hopeful moment, like many others, faded over the subsequent days and eventually disappeared completely. I'm not even sure if he remembered what he promised us that day, breaking the already fragile trust of his children once more.

The following years seemed like a broken record, falling into a sickening routine. Either my father was working abroad or on a business trip. Those were the moments when I didn't have to worry about being hit again. From Monday to Wednesday, life was in a state of limbo, a brief respite from tension. By Thursday, I felt the anxiety creeping back, and by Friday, it completely consumed me.

Weekends were hellish. While other kids rested and recharged for the upcoming school week, for me, it was the opposite. My father would return home, expecting to find the ideal children he had always dreamed of, not the ones who continuously fell short of his expectations. He found reasons to hit us for just about anything, always claiming it was our fault. Again, I felt that I deserved it. Weekends went by as usual, with an increasing aversion to life and an emotional paralysis slowly dragging my soul down. The constant visits to Grandma's, the shared meals, and my father's never-ending complaining. Shame. Pain. Emptiness.

Countless times, I believed that my father could change, and I clung to those words with hope. Why wouldn't I? When a parent inflicts violence upon a child, the child's love for themselves diminishes first, not the love for the parent. Over time, all I felt was fear, yet for many years, I believed he must have had a reason for his actions. As I grew older, it became clear that I was merely a vent for his frustrations and it had nothing to do with him trying to raise a competent human being. He betrayed my already fragile trust in him so many times that it's hard for me to say whether I could believe in any future that wasn't as bleak as the image of the next day.

When we inherit our worldview from our parents

Our behavior originates from certain patterns that our parents lived by and which they also adopted from their families. The mind is inherently lazy, and mimicking other people's behavior provides it with the simplest path, offering the most comfort. Until we realize that we can alter this dynamic, we'll perpetuate this behavior, falling into the same reactionary patterns, and believing what we're conditioned to believe. This can make us feel like the greatest victims of life. It's only natural for a child to mimic their parents' behavior and perspective rather than heed their words. Of course, much depends on the individual child and the strength of their character. However, it's challenging to show love to oneself and others if it's absent from one's home environment. This absence might also lead to clumsiness and a lack of life structure, as well as a disinclination for confronting personal problems, choosing to blame everyone else but oneself instead. While this may be a sign of immaturity in adults, in children, it often stems from stress and a lack of foundational support.

My father belonged to a family that one could categorize as deeply unhappy. Their mindset was tainted with toxicity, displaying maladaptive reactions to their surroundings and harboring beliefs that, to this day, I find incomprehensible. Physical punishment and humiliation were their regular, simplest, and most effective tools for any issue. Their complete lack of guilt, combined with their propensity to place blame on everyone around them, was second nature to them. Throughout his life, my father felt victimized. Initially by his mother, and subsequently by his wife and children. His life was an endless cycle of complaints, finger-pointing, and enforcing obedience through physical and verbal aggression. He wasn't interested in genuine connection, just a contrived form of respect. Whenever something went against his vision of our behavior, he turned into our tormentor.

My mother, like me, had a strained relationship with her mother-in-law. It's hardly surprising, given that the latter deemed my mother entirely unworthy of her son. The irony of this situation was that she herself did not see her son as deserving of praise or love. Therefore, she prevented him from bonding with anyone who might potentially offer what she would not. I suspect that any potential wife for my father would have faced a similar disdain and hostility. Unfortunately, or perhaps fortunately, it was my mother who bore the brunt of such an attitude. Could their relationship have ever worked? It's hard to say whether they could ever have come to a mutual understanding. One thing's for sure: a person who believes the world owes them simply for existing is ludicrous. And if they also view themselves as a perpetual victim because the world doesn't align with their viewpoint, they become a caricature. It's just a pity that the focus of their action is on getting revenge on their innocent children.

Perhaps that's why he nipped in the bud every endeavor I undertook that set me apart, every dream and behavior that could threaten his twisted vision. I wasn't allowed to have a boyfriend. I couldn't dress as I wanted, and any potential friends had to be filtered through his arbitrary approval. My needs for intimacy, creativity, love, or even the simple desire to voice my own opinion were suppressed and trampled upon. All he would say was how ashamed he was of us. When I wrote my first love letter, he took it from me, shouting that I was a "skank." If I remember correctly, it was a simple, innocent Valentine's letter that we would send anonymously within our class. Only the recipient's name was on the envelope, inside of which was a drawing expressing fondness. Another such incident took place when I was preparing a holiday gift for a classmate in a gift exchange. I wanted to give the person a creatively crafted card with artificial snow, a Christmas tree, and pieces of broken ornaments as decorations. Unfortunately, both my Valentine and the card were trampled upon. I wasn't allowed to do such things; I had no right to express myself in my unique way.

I was a child filled with hope and lofty emotions, like any other, yet he persistently dragged me down to his level, explaining that sex, love, tenderness, or even mere interest in the opposite sex were disgusting and that I had no right to even think about it, let alone act upon such feelings.

I close my eyes as I recall the meaning of the word "shame". And how deeply he made me feel it firsthand. I'm convinced he didn't know and still doesn't understand what true shame is. In essence, it's fear. He probably doesn't remember how much he let me down when he was drunk and I led him home until he lost his balance and fell into a dumpster. Did I have the strength to do that as a first-grade student? I must have. Did he feel shame when he mindlessly urinated off the balcony? Was he embarrassed about his lack of hygiene, which resulted in him losing his front teeth? Did he feel regret and shame toward his little child, my tiny sister when he caused her to become dangerously dehydrated? Did he feel that he was hurting someone? Did he feel the responsibility he had on his shoulders, which he was never able to bear? That's what shame was. The fact that he couldn't manage at any stage of his parenthood and life. And that he still can't understand that he is not the victim.

It's hard to let go of resentment toward those who painted a distorted image of the world to a child who wanted to eagerly embrace it. It's challenging to understand that the world is different and that one can truly achieve anything one sets their mind to, regardless of the starting point we're given. It's a prolonged, arduous journey, one that we usually undertake only in adulthood. Sometimes, there never comes a moment when one re-

alizes they don't have to live like their parents did. Anyone can always change, but they also need to understand that such change demands effort. The more we aim to alter false, hurtful beliefs about ourselves, our environment, and others in our lives, the more challenging it becomes.

When Skipping School Becomes a Crime

Sometimes in life, we do things we feel like doing, which might not necessarily align with generally accepted norms. Occasionally, we might inadvertently hurt someone without having any malicious intent. It's favorable when we naturally face the consequences and learn a valuable lesson without further harming others. It becomes problematic, however, when someone tries to convince us that our behavior is a failure. That what we've done and achieved represents our great defeat. A self-aware person knows that there's no such thing as pure failure—only lessons.

From what I recall, I played hooky when I was about nine or ten. I didn't go behind a kiosk to drink or hang out by a nearby building. Instead, I took a stroll to Malbork. I enjoyed the beautiful weather while observing the castle and its surroundings. It was just bad luck that my mother happened to see me the moment I boarded the bus. It hadn't occurred to me to get on at the next stop because I didn't think it would be an issue at all. I spent a peaceful, relatively neutral day, but eventually, I had to return. And I did, without giving it much thought.

The day came when my father returned from a business trip. My mother called me into the kitchen and narrated the entire episode to him. As a naive child who still had a smidge of faith in her parents, I smiled gently, thinking of my little escapade as a trivial matter. Without inquiring about the details or reasons for missing school, I was beaten. They didn't care about why I did it. I was punished, and that was supposed to be the end of it; I was not to do it again. No more discussions, in which I had no active participation. At that moment, I felt I was punished more for my smile than for skipping school.

I remember him sitting by the window and smoking. As long as my mother was talking, he didn't move, but when she finished and I smiled, he rapidly got up from his chair, put out the cigarette and grabbed me by the arm. He dragged me into the room and, not letting me go, he pulled a belt out of the cabinet and started to beat me all over my body. Afterward, he told me to go to my room. My mother was quietly sitting in the kitchen throughout the whole thing, and I literally couldn't walk, because I was staggering with pain. I was crying so hard that I couldn't breathe, I was just wailing. I was also bewildered, as I couldn't understand what had just happened.

At that moment, I wanted to die. My father was beating me for a very long time, and I was just letting my mind go numb, as I wanted it to end. I fervently hoped he would just kill me. What did I have to live for? Was there anything worth enough for me to stay? Was there anyone who would miss me? The pain was piercing, but it was hard for me to tell whether it was the ache in my body or heartache. I didn't know where he was hitting me and with what, as I was dazed. He must have been in a state of pathological ecstasy or fury, because what he did to me then was horrifying. He was blindly hitting my arms, legs, and buttocks, and his beating left me with bruises that didn't go away for quite some time. He was hitting my eyes, which I couldn't open after that. And my head, which caused me to vomit a lot... To this day I have some marks that remind me of that moment. The scars that he has left on my back and my soul.

When he finally finished, every part of my body was aching, feeling both excruciating pain and emptiness. I had no one to turn to for solace, no one embraced me, no one helped me up. I didn't want a father capable of doing that to me. That day, he stripped away my last traces of trust in people. I desperately wished that someone at school could see the state I was in. Maybe someone would notice and take me to a children's home? I simply yearned to feel safe. The mere thought of being unwanted felt far-fetched, but at that moment, it was the only thing keeping me from total despair.

The next morning, I woke up with a bitten tongue. Due to the injuries from the night before, I suffered my first epileptic seizure. I felt drained, with dizziness consuming me, and I could hardly walk. After having something for breakfast, I fell asleep again. I woke up in the evening, had dinner, and sleep quickly overcame me once more. The subsequent morning, I overheard my father mumbling about my condition. Did he worry I might die? Did he consider that this was the result of his actions? I doubt he was genuinely concerned about my well-being. It's more likely he was afraid he might face legal consequences. In any case, they packed me into the car and took me to my paternal grandmother, Helena. She deduced that my seizures weren't the result of the trauma or any illness, but that I was possessed by the devil. This was only two days after the beating, and the mere journey was painful for me. They seemed oblivious to that fact. I recall my father complaining about the inconvenience my condition had caused him, as he'd now have to see a doctor. This entire ordeal fueled my hopes of dying the next time my father laid his hands on me. For days, I lived with the notion that I was possessed and would soon die, freeing me from the enduring pain I felt.

I remember an instance that depicted the fear I felt toward my father nearly every day during my childhood. I was about thirteen, and during a walk with a boy I had a crush on, he gave me a hickey. My fear of my father was so paralyzing that I tried to hide it by burning the mark with an iron. I wanted a blister to form over the spot, disregarding the pain. And even though he's now far away from me, devoid of any physical or mental strength to harm me, I still fear him like that little girl did. I feel I must come to terms with the past and move forward. Voicing these words alone feels liberating, lightening the weight that had been pressing down on me.

Did all of this stop me from skipping school again? Far from it. The epileptic seizure unleashed a profound anxiety within me. Every place felt unbearable, and stimuli seemed to assault me from every direction. This constant sense of overstimulation was draining. Hence, I would often skip classes to retreat to the forest. Only there did I feel safe. There, I could find peace and momentarily forget what my father did to me and what I lacked. I was alone there—without noise and people. This need for solitude became deeply ingrained in me, to the point where, over time, I began to feel no need for others' company. I increasingly distanced myself from the world, creating a space just for myself. That's how it remains to this day. It was just easier that way.

Today, what brings me relief is undeniably the forest and its ambiance. A solitary walk, with only my thoughts for company, rejuvenates my body and mind, clears my head, and allows me to take a deep, healthy breath. Perhaps this feeling started during that time when I discovered the woods as a perfect escape. Even though I now enjoy being alone, I've gained an awareness I didn't have back then. We shouldn't run from negative emotions; instead, we should understand and release them. We can't avoid people forever; we need them for building relationships, growth, and energy exchange. So, what could I have been feeling back then when I didn't know any of this? I suppressed my emotions, suffocating them further inside me. Piling up issues, the lack of an outlet for negative energy, and loneliness created a state I still struggle to escape from. However, I know I'm on the right path now.

When guilt becomes the heaviest burden in life

Self-worth is something that guides our entire lives. If a young child doesn't feel valued, lacks support, and faces criticism for everything they do, they won't be able to rise above it. Childhood will transition into adulthood, where they'll seek validation for every action from others, overlooking their needs and self-worth. We can't live for others without granting ourselves the realization that we are enough. However, if everyone close to the child tells them that their life and actions are wrong and contemptible, they will accept this "truth" as painful but natural. They'll internalize it as a foundation, seeing themselves as a worthless reject of the world.

Another moment, when words became something like a foundation to me, was an incident that took place at my friend's house. I was in my second year of middle school, so I was about fifteen. I remember that her family had a guest. There was alcohol, and the guest did not shy away from it. At one point he offered me sex for money. He told me about this meetup in flowery language. The icky words and the wandering eyes of an adult man who crosses a child's personal boundaries are imprinted on my memory.

His wandering eyes, skeevy smile, and confidence have been based on a sick perception of reality. I was shocked, I waited until he finished speaking, and quickly told my friend what had happened, and she, in turn, told her mom. This way my parents were the next to find out. When my father came back from Germany, he heard about this incident, but his reaction was far from that of a normal parent. My friend's mom called him and told him they needed to meet. I was sitting nearby when she told him the details and I waited for his reaction. After hearing the story, he jokingly wagged the finger as if at the man who wanted to have sex with his daughter. I was so disappointed. He told me that I had probably provoked him and it was all my fault. It turned out that I was asking for such things to happen to me, that I deserved them.

"How much money have you made on that?" he asked venomously, and then he hit me in the face several times.

I remember that he told me all this on the way home. We passed by the field where my schoolmates were playing soccer. I also saw a few adults standing by. My father didn't mind their presence and pulled my hair and kicked me several times right there. I don't know if anyone noticed that, or saw it and ignored it, or if I was invisible. No one shouted at my father to stop. Maybe he would come to his senses? A thirty-year-old man was hitting a fifteen-year-old girl with her head down. I didn't even lift it, and when I felt that he was kicking me again, I prayed for someone to help me. Can't anyone see me? Will someone scream at him to stop? Don't I really mean anything to anyone?

This was the moment when I believed that I was the source of all my problems. Not others. That night I couldn't sleep, holding my burning cheeks and searching my thoughts for the moment when I provoked that man to make such a proposal. I wanted to remind myself of what I had done so that I wouldn't repeat it. From then on, my sense of worth disappeared, and I believed I was a particularly hopeless case.

All my childhood, I heard, mainly from him, that I was to blame for everything that happened. So, I was to blame for my father hitting me, or for him arguing with a neighbor. All situations that couldn't be explained right away must have been caused by my bad behavior, and every response and word from me was a hurtful lie and terrible insubordination. I had no right to react differently than he expected, and if I did, I was ungrateful and obstinate. I was to blame for every misfortune in his life, and I had brought this fate upon myself. I could have been exactly as he wanted me to be. However, I dare to doubt if that would have changed anything, or if he would simply move on to his manipulations, creating another sick reality in which he continued to poison my mind with his toxic beliefs.

I knew then that I was alone in the world. That I am and will be insignificant to anyone. That I can't trust anyone. That I'm not worth befriending. That I am not worthy of love. That nobody cares about me.

It's right to feel responsible for everything that happens around us. When we believe that agency is in our hands, and all we have to do is act. An adult may feel fear and pain, but cannot expect someone to fix it. We are responsible for our safety, emotions, feelings, and the mentioned agency. Fear without a sense of agency, waiting for help, and lacking the courage to act is the domain of children and immature people. A child in whose life there is no support or trust, will not know how to reach out for help on their own. It's even harder when they either don't know how to do it, or don't receive support even from official entities. Of course, society's reaction to a child's suffering should be consistent. A child should receive sup-

port precisely because they might not know that they desperately need help. So if a child doesn't get help, they will live alone, grow up alone, and repeat patterns until they want to live differently. Sadly, this doesn't happen as often as it should.

When Alcohol Takes the Lead

Addiction is a disease. Regardless of the object of addiction, it isn't something we inherently need in life. In our mind, it may seem as essential as air, but due to the disease, we can't think clearly. Why would we stop when using alcohol, drugs, or other dangerous substances makes us feel better? Why quit when the absence of these substances causes irritation, frustration, or even anger and aggression in us? Why change something that gives us pleasure?

A particularly memorable moment for me regarding my father's alcoholism was when we were at his friend's plot in what is commonly known as community gardens. I was eight years old. While he continued to get drunk, I played with the other kids. However, there came a point when the party was over. It was summer, so it got dark quite late, but we left around midnight. I had to guide him home. I remember that to move him, I had to stand behind him, place my hands on his back, and push him. We went through the entire neighborhood this way. At one point, my school teacher came out onto her balcony and saw my father fall beside the trash bins. Our eyes met, and then she went back inside and turned off her lights. Shaking off that moment of embarrassment, I began to lift my father. Fortunately, I managed. The next day, my mother laughingly recounted how he returned from the party and urinated over the balcony, allowing all our neighbors to see the state he was in when his daughter dragged him home.

One day, he woke up hungover and decided to drink some water mixed with syrup. He forgot that my mother often poured dishwashing liquid into empty syrup bottles. He grabbed one such bottle and drank its contents.

He found the situation hilariously amusing, joking that he would be blowing bubbles.

Another incident that's deeply ingrained in my memory happened when I was about five or six. He liked taking me out for a beer then. We had an arrangement: for every beer he bought for himself, he would buy me a treat. It could be pretzel sticks, peanuts, or any other snack available at the bar or store. We were in a bar, and when he went to the restroom, I took a sip of his beer. I was tiny, sitting on a high bar stool. At some point, I must've felt dizzy because I began rocking back and forth on it. Eventually, I fell and began to cry profusely. He rushed from the restroom to handle the situation. Initially, he consoled me, but moments later, he began yelling at me. I remember feeling awful, and the fact that he forbade me to tell anyone made it even worse. We sat in that bar for another hour before heading straight home.

I don't recall anyone ever confronting him about his drinking. For the people around us, it seemed to be a source of amusement, but I felt isolated. Kids didn't want to play with someone whose father would urinate off a balcony in front of everyone.

I still remember another, perhaps the only positive thing associated with my father's drinking. One day, when he came home drunk, I asked him if we could get a dog. My friend was giving away a few puppies at the time, and I wanted one. My father quickly agreed on the condition that I clean my room. I did so without hesitation, and the next day, I excitedly went to get my reddish puppy. When I brought him home, my father began to yell at me. Scared, I reminded him that he had agreed the day before. And that's how Dollar became a part of our family. I took care of him the best I could – feeding him, walking him, and bathing him, showering him with love. He was with us for four years before he was tragically hit by a friend's car. The driver didn't even stop to see what happened, and of course, later denied it.

My mother was familiar with the issue of alcohol from her family home.

She could joke about it around my father, but she had to be aware of how serious it was, as she began to educate herself on the topic. Initially, she might have tried to hide this, but she wasn't very discreet about it. One day, she bought a book on alcoholics, and my father found it. Being an "expert" on every subject, he had something to say about it. He boasted about knowing exactly what would be happening next and what my mother would try to implement in her life to get him out of his so-called addiction. I remember she once asked him to attend AA meetings, and to my surprise, he agreed.

By then, I knew he had an alcohol problem. No person who handles alcohol well acts the way he did, or the way other people with similar issues act. Every day after his trips abroad, the stack of beer bottles kept growing. He was drunk at my First Communion and every family gathering, and I even remember him drinking with my mother's father. There's no doubt he was a full-blown alcoholic.

He did attend AA meetings, but after the second one, he claimed the leader asked him why he was even there since he didn't have an alcohol problem. This raises questions – was he lying to us or during therapy? Even a stranger would find it hard to believe he was a healthy individual. This was glaringly obvious. Even I could see it as a young child.

Interestingly, my father often resorted to lies. He used them as a daily tool to achieve his immediate goals. But I was the one constantly called a liar. It didn't matter if I was being truthful. If something didn't align with his views, I was the one twisting reality. In truth, he couldn't cope with life, and unfortunately, my mother, myself, and others around him bore the brunt of it. He was a master manipulator, always supported by his equally flawed parents. Despite attending AA meetings, not much changed. At one point, he had a heart attack which should have been a wake-up call. But just two or three weeks later, he was drinking again. He even joked that non-alcoholic beer costs the same as regular beer, so he didn't see the point in buying it.

When he was drunk, he was more humane, much gentler. He would let me do pretty much anything. I could go to a party or ask his permission for something else. I wasn't as scared of him then, so I preferred him drunk.

Seeing all these situations, I soon began to drink myself. The first time I got drunk was on Christmas Eve. I might have been only twelve, and I could barely stand during the midnight Mass. That same year, on New Year's Eve, I got even more intoxicated. The next day I felt terrible. When I began drinking regularly, my body reacted poorly. The day after, I always felt sick, couldn't concentrate on my lessons, and struggled to function normally.

When betrayals come into play

A lack of trust in one's parents is something unimaginable. When a child can't find fundamental security at home, when they can't trust their father and mother with their life, they are not only lonely but also deprived of a chance for proper emotional development. When they additionally see that the parents don't trust each other and hide various situations from one another, the child becomes even more lost.

When my mother was pregnant with her first child and up until she became pregnant with the second, she lived in a convent center in Krakow. Later, when my father finally managed to find some accommodations, we moved there, and my mother began planning her return to work once we started daycare and preschool. At that moment, Helena stepped in with an irresistible offer. She persuaded my father to move with us to Sztum, as she got a mortgage and purchased an apartment there. My father probably had no objections, but my mother had many. She had a circle of friends in Krakow and truly wanted to return to work. Eventually, she was given an ultimatum: either stay in Krakow and return to the convent or leave with my father.

From the stories, I know that the costs, which were much lower in Sztum, played a role in this decision.

I was five years old, and I remember we were already living in Sztum. One day, my father took us with him to Krakow. We went without my mother. On the way, we stopped in a town near Krakow. My father decided to spend the night with a female friend. That time, he woke us up while he was having sex with her. Sadly, this was typical, and this was the reality we lived in. My parents constantly cheated on each other, seemingly seeing nothing wrong in it. So, when my father later reproached my mother for her visits to prison, she reminded him of his lady friend from Krakow. Of course, he didn't see anything wrong with it. He said it was just sex and that it wasn't important. During one of these conversations, my father also mentioned for the first time that Helena, his mother, was cheated on by her husband her whole life and she wasn't indifferent to it.

Maybe that's what made her become such a repellent person. Allegedly, she wanted to divorce him, but out of consideration for their two children and the times they lived in, she ultimately decided against it. She regretted it till the end. My father must have taken an example from his life, treating sex and betrayals as a mere everyday occurrence. So what if it was dirty, unjust, and hurt others? According to him, that's just how life was, and why should he fight against it or, even more so, search for any guilt within himself?

Grandpa used to hit Helena as well as his two sons, who sometimes also got it from their not-entirely stable mother. So, my father served his family a repeat performance, using his childhood as the primary foundation for building the future. I know from stories told by his childhood friends that he often appeared dirty, snotty, in torn clothes, and hungry. They lived so frugally, not because they had to, but because they wanted to have as much money in the bank as possible. They spent the bare minimum, failing to provide either for their children or themselves any basics for a normal life. This doesn't excuse my father's actions, but it sheds some light on the reasons he treated us the way he did later on.

Both my parents perpetuated the patterns from their dysfunctional families, completely oblivious to the harm they were doing to each other and their children. They lived in this chaos like the blind, with no plan or direction in life. Today, I feel like a puzzle piece that doesn't fit. Those times were challenging for many reasons, and the lack of awareness that we can and should change harmful beliefs rooted in our childhood doomed the happiness of many kids. I'm glad I didn't fit into that world, although I still struggle to understand why I ended up in a place where I didn't belong at all. In any sense.

Therapy became my tool for mending my soul and what transpired during my childhood. According to one theory, the Soul chooses a specific incarnation to undergo lessons and evolve. From this perspective, I'm grateful that I managed to rise above and live on the surface. Still, I wish I could live as I do now without carrying the weight on my back that just won't let go. I believe many things would come much more easily to me.

My father had the incredible and most damaging support from his mother, Helena, which hurt others and, most of all, himself. It was so inappropriate that thinking about it now brings a hollow laugh to my lips. The beliefs Helena ingrained in him must've distorted his view of reality and certainly laid the groundwork for his adulthood. She convinced him that he was the only valuable person in his family and that his job gave him authority and power over us. She instilled in him disdain for us and our mother, and all this fell on fertile ground. Therefore, our mother was on the receiving end of vindictiveness and venomous remarks. She was poorly educated, came from a bad family, and didn't live up to Helena's expectations. After my parents divorced, my father got involved with a woman who had a higher education than my mother and was a teacher.

There was a grating feeling inside me when Helena said my father always deserved a woman like Nina. In contrast, I cheekily retorted that they didn't match, as my father couldn't string a correct sentence together while Nina taught small children such elementary skills. I tried defending my mother this way, who, in Helena's eyes and words, was always seen as a lesser woman.

My father, in his childhood, must have been repeatedly mentally broken, or he was inherently weak in this realm, because despite the harm done to him in his early years, the lack of love, respect, and understanding, he still blindly believed everything his mother told him. Helena's husband was somewhat different, but he always took my father's side. For them, it was unthinkable that anyone might have a bad opinion of him. He worked, earned money, and therefore had the right to live exactly as he wanted. What did it matter that he took away our right to happiness? Because of such support, he always had someone to turn to with his imagined concerns, always someone confirming that he was right. There was no chance for a light bulb moment for him, realizing it was time to change, not only for his family's sake but also for himself. Unfortunately, in my opinion, there was no room for that.

Returning to Nina, the woman my father got involved with... For fifteen years, she probably didn't find out about how he beat us, intimidated us, and harmed us in nearly every aspect of life. At least not from him. This fact is both astonishing and horrifying to me. Nina teaches grades one through three. Such a person should be full of empathy, understanding, and compassion. Has it never occurred to her that something might be off when his children don't want any contact with him? She never delved into the reason for this and remains in a relationship built on alarming lies, half-truths, and harm to others. Did she never care that her partner disregarded his children? Was there never a moment when a red warning light flicked on in her mind, prompting her to ask us, especially when she didn't get answers from her partner? How smitten must she have been with my father? Perhaps he told her his version of events, distorted by what he has or rather had in his mind, and she blindly believed him, simultaneously downgrading us to deceitful, ungrateful beings. It's incredible that in her eyes, everyone else was wrong, but her partner was right. So, in my mind, I can lump her with Helena or into an even worse category whose depths I don't even want to fathom. Remember, she's a teacher of young children. What values could she impart to them?

Agata has been undergoing psychiatric treatment for many years, and he played no part in that. Damian was in prison and later became homeless, and his whereabouts are currently unknown.

When a Father Rejects His Child

A child is born with an inherent need to belong to their close kin. If they are rejected, they lose their grounding. It's hard to understand individuals who deprive their children of love, daily affection, and a genuine childhood. It raises the question: should everyone become a parent in their lifetime? Perhaps there should be a selection process, examining whether an individual can provide a child with the necessities or impart the fundamental values needed for a regular, healthy existence.

I'm primarily referring to those times when he pushed me away. He did the same to my sister and brother. Currently, my sister has not been in contact with him for several years. It all began when he kicked her out of the house. She was living with him at the time and started developing anxieties and social phobias. As a result, she stopped attending school but never confided in him about it.

One day, my father didn't go to work because he had a doctor's appointment, and he discovered that I hadn't gone to school. Word by word, he found out that I hadn't been attending for some time, and he bluntly told me to get the hell out and go to my mother's. Of course, I left and never contacted him again.

Today, he completely doesn't understand it. To him, his behavior is natural, and his daughter should understand rather than distance herself. For him, the situation is incomprehensible, and he feels victimized. He's told me many times about how he was treated the same way by Helena and that it was a survival lesson for him, not a reason to cut ties. He sees this method as a valuable parenting tool and sees nothing wrong with it. That's why he replicated it with his children, us.

Throughout my life, I encountered these situations. I remember when I stopped going to school; he told me to change my last name, saying that since I wasn't studying, I was no longer a Gitszel. Most of the time, it was about school or friends he didn't like. When I said I would continue seeing them regardless, the kindest thing he'd say was that he was ashamed of me. Several times in adulthood, he told me not to identify as his daughter. Now, I feel a bit lighter because therapy helped me regain my balance. I don't want to see him, call him, or explain things to him. I always felt he was a bit less sharp than me, and explaining my feelings when he spoke to me in certain ways seemed pointless.

During my younger years, I encountered many situations related to my father's rejection. Today, it still hurts a bit, but I have significantly distanced myself from him, and it's hard to say if I harbor any warm feelings toward him. When he calls, I don't feel love and I struggle to recognize him as my father. Emotionally, he's entirely alien to me. The only familial bond I feel is with my mother, but it mostly stems from my sympathy for her challenging childhood and later toxic marriage with my father.

I'm not trying to excuse anyone, but I strive to understand that my parents' childhoods significantly influenced their worldview and adulthood. Sadly, they never realized that one could live and raise children differently than they were taught. Thankfully, I understood that before my sons were born.

Helena

When a Father's Mother Wants to Be the Most Important

Grandparents are associated with warmth, unconditional love, security, and support that's unparalleled. They're often connected with memories of carefree vacations, wiping away childhood tears, and answering the never-ending questions of little ones. Grandparents are the people you run to with problems, and they always find time for you. At least, in an ideal world.

In my case, I do remember several safe years when my maternal grandparents would come to look after me. Basia and Henio gave me a taste of a real childhood. Sadly, this soon ended, and my father's mother permanently stepped in. Helena, a cold woman devoid of any grandmotherly traits, was a devout Catholic who always taught me what she believed I should know and say. Most of it was church-related. I recall the ever-present Radio Maryja and her passionately reciting the rosary. I remember learning the rosary and attending May devotions.

I often visited her during holidays, weekends, and vacations. I loved going there. The pond, river, beautiful forests, and fields gave me a pleasant sense of tranquility, especially after time at home. Few houses and a break from everyday stress. Sunday dinners at Grandma's were a sacred tradition for my father. During these dinners, she'd boast about her supposed wealth and complain about others, mocking them, for example, for having just a plain chicken soup on Sundays. A few houses down lived my mother's parents, whom my father's family deemed inferior in every aspect.

I still struggle to understand the difference between my mother's and father's parents. Both grandfathers drank, and neither household was affluent. Perhaps the distinction came from my father's parents believing their apartments were clear signs of wealth. Indeed, they had four apartments, but they were in poor condition and simply stolen. During the time of the State Agricultural Farms (PGR) in Poland, my grandma worked in an office and just took them for herself. As a child, I didn't have much say, and the constant indoctrination that they were better, even if I didn't fully believe it, eventually had its effects. I was confused but also inclined to believe that on some level, my father's parents were better than my mother's. This deeply instilled in me the belief that to be better, I needed to have a lot of money. In one conversation, I learned that a certain percentage of people in the world are unemployed, and I began to worry immensely. That it would be me who wouldn't find a job, that I'd be jobless and penniless, and therefore worse than others. That I wouldn't be a valuable person.

Everything Helena told me, I deeply analyzed and simultaneously doubted. Some of her words I didn't believe at all, yet some of them found fertile ground, from which my perception of reality vigorously sprouted. I remember what linked my father and Helena. Namely, the lack of answers to a child's tough questions, of which I had many. Once, as we walked down the street and saw a cleaning lady, Grandma told me that if I didn't study, I'd end up like her. It was meant to strike and straighten me out, but I simply didn't see anything wrong with cleaning.

"Someone has to clean for it to be tidy, right?" I asked without hesitation. "What's wrong with that?"

Of course, I received no answer, just a particular look and a grimace that my father also made in such situations. Both would characteristically lift one part of their upper lip, and I remember how much I disliked that. Such a strong memory that they genuinely did not know the answers to some of my questions. Typically, those answers would require them to show empathy toward another person, like the cleaning lady who was just doing her job. A necessary, hard job.

Helena felt superior to others and never missed an opportunity to remind me of it. The Church gave her something to believe in and spread. She clung to its rules, generally looking down on others who lived differently.

She never spoke of her mistakes and flaws. She also never mentioned that Grandpa cheated on her. That told me a lot about her behavior. I learned this from my father when I was an adult. I was pregnant with my second child when he got drunk. I learned that Grandpa had cheated on her all his life, not caring about her feelings or thoughts.

Clearly, in my family, feminine energies were and are very disturbed, and this had a significant impact on shaping my personality. Grandma treated me like a punching bag, probably because she couldn't handle her love for me or any relationship with the female part of my life. She always dreamt of the city but had to stay in the countryside and work hard. She faced various diseases, yet she yearned for life. But completely different than the one she had.

In the countryside, at least in mine, no one ever told anyone anything negative to their face, but all the grievances were vented among themselves, at home. However, one day, the mother of a girl came to my grandma with news. Earlier, her daughter had gone to my grandpa with something to return to him. When she arrived and handed it over, Grandpa wanted a kiss on the lips, which made her run away screaming, immediately reporting the situation to her mother. The woman took her daughter and went to confront my grandpa. She first asked him what had happened and then sternly warned him never to do that again. He not only scared the child but could have traumatized her. She said she wouldn't ignore this, to which Helena reacted peculiarly.

"Did something like that happen? He just wanted a kiss!" she seemed utterly unfazed by the situation, which the woman immediately pointed out.

"It looks like you're used to this. People know things, even if they don't talk about them. I won't stay silent about this."

I only learned about this recently, but then some of my memories took on a terrifying meaning. I remember that one day when I was watching a Polish TV series with them, Grandpa sat next to me for the

47

entire episode. Very close, his hand on my knee. I felt uncomfortable and often just moved away or sat a bit farther. I don't know if he tried something, but my reaction thwarted any plans he might have had.

Helena also had a very strained relationship with my mother. She belittled her at every opportunity, treating her as if she were an inferior human being. She believed and openly communicated that my mother wasn't a good wife for her son. She disapproved of the fact that my mom came from a poor family and hadn't attended a prestigious school. These were the two most common reasons for criticizing her. The fact that my mom had finished a painting technical school seemed laughable and even demeaning to Helena. It didn't matter that my mother chose that path for practical reasons or that my father attended the same school. My father later graduated from an electrical technical school, and Helena saw that as proof that he was simply better than my mother.

In my opinion, a person's school and education should never define their worth. However, Helena's opinions unfortunately affected my perspective for a long time. I remember my father once proudly saying that his mother had a tractor driver's license. This fact became a tool for me, helping me cope when Helena hurled insults my way. The fact that she couldn't live as she wanted and further limited her femininity by driving a tractor made me feel superior to her. Whenever there was tension between us, I would think to myself, "Just go ride your tractor," and it always lifted my spirits.

Reflecting on how my father's mother behaved and lived, it's clear she hid her husband and son's wrongdoings from everyone. She fiercely defended them. She never reported any of my grandfather's misdeeds, and she defended her son even when he was clearly at fault. She always blamed my mother first, then me, and sometimes even my uncle's wife. She constantly emphasized that hard work was the only virtue and the key to success. Putting others down was a daily routine for her. I now realize that all of this was a façade to hide her profound unhappiness.

Later, when my childhood home became vacant for various reasons, she moved in. When I was an adult visiting her, she would often ask me about my life, bragging about how well she had set up her new place. She'd boast about living in the city and how convenient everything was. She saved money, and her living conditions were excellent. She believed she had earned all this from her hard work in the countryside. She couldn't comprehend that living in a town of fifteen thousand people was nothing like city life. I never felt like arguing or explaining it to her. There was no point. She was delusional in believing she achieved all this on her own. However, one day, I couldn't hold back and suggested she visit me.

"I'd love to go to Gdansk and see what you're actually doing there," she provocatively said. I took the bait and replied:

"Well, pack your bags, Helena, and come over. I'd love to show you around." She didn't respond, so I added: "You'll quickly notice the difference. Just wait until you have to pay rent here. One month of rent here could last you two, maybe even three months back home."

Once again, she didn't reply, just made her usual disdainful face. She might not have admitted it, but I know I struck a chord.

Another memory of her stands out in my mind. I think I was in fifth grade when it happened. We were planning some renovations, and during that time, we didn't know where to keep our pet rabbit. My father asked her if she could take care of it for a couple of weeks, to which she agreed. As a child, I never suspected anything bad could happen. We visited her one weekend, and it turned out she had put our domesticated rabbit outside in a cage with hares during winter. When I heard this, I was in disbelief. How could she be so thoughtless? I rushed to see my rabbit, but it was already dead. I returned, tears in my eyes.

"Grandma, why did you do this? Can't you tell the difference between a pet and a wild animal?"

She muttered something under her breath. When I cried, she said:

"You should be crying over your grades, not some rabbit."

At that moment, I felt like showing emotion over the loss of a pet was futile. It felt like a cruel lesson for me to focus on my studies and not care about trivial things. This incident haunted me for years, and I confronted her about it when she lived in her "luxurious" city apartment. She initially pretended not to remember, but I persisted. She tried to complain to my father, but by then, he had no control over me. I realized she lacked basic human emotions, and her lack of emotional development was significant. Helena burdened me with harmful, hurtful, and heavy stereotypes. She harmed her loved ones without batting an eye, while self-righteously placing herself on a pedestal. She was utterly egocentric and a hypocrite. Helena shook my faith in myself and my entire world, especially through her unwavering support of her son, who would lay hands on me.

Because of her words, I felt worthless and undeserving of my father's love for a long time. I hated myself and always felt inadequate. I never allowed myself to make mistakes, and new situations terrified me. I despised taking risks. This mindset eventually led me to alcohol, which temporarily numbed the pain of feeling rejected.

People can endure anything if they view such experiences as lessons, but it's hard for a child to do so. A child absorbs the world as it's presented. They crave closeness, and when they're consistently denied love and understanding, they perceive the world as distorted, cruel, harsh, and unfriendly. No child should ever feel this way, even once. Yet, that's how I felt throughout my childhood, adolescence, and early adulthood.

When words hurt just as much as actions

We don't like being criticized, and hurtful remarks are something that raises our guard and often incites aggression. Excessive control from others is usually frustrating, and having our mistakes pointed out or hearing unnecessary advice turns life into a battlefield. What if our childhood was full of understanding and patience? What if our mother or father had the strength to tell us why they think we're doing something wrong, or why we can't touch a hot pot? Perhaps receiving someone's comments would be easier and above all constructive. When a small child constantly hears messages like Leave it! Don't break that! Calm down! Stop! You can't do it! I'm ashamed of you! Why aren't you like other children? Why are you doing that again? Can't you just be quiet? I don't care! Stop crying! – then they won't build any valuable foundations for themselves. Such a child doesn't believe that they are loved and that they can meet life's challenges. Such a child feels that they shouldn't exist.

Helena never raised a hand against me, but she often tried to hurt me in other ways. She would say things meant to hurt me and often succeeded. When she saw that I reacted too gently or was not affected by what she said, she would attack harder and faster until she achieved her intended goal. She must've noticed when she succeeded because when I felt humiliated or sad, she would let up with satisfaction. She often told me fabricated stories about her life that I somewhat doubted, and when I asked too many questions, she would lose her temper.

I remember when I was seven years old, she decided to give me a dress. She searched in her closet for a while and eventually pulled out a slightly crumpled item. It was a very pretty, flowy midi dress. Yellow, with ruffles and some faded red elements. I remember really liking it. It was July, my name day, but I don't particularly remember any emotions from that day other than the happiness I felt at that moment. I thanked her for the dress, put it on, and quickly went outside. I wore it without objection, more out of habit since refusing Grandma wasn't something allowed in my family. Luckily for me, I didn't feel like refusing that day.

Later, I went for a walk around the neighborhood. At one point, I sat on a bench next to a neighbor who bluntly informed me that I stank.

"Where did you get that dress, girl?" she asked with a wrinkled nose.

"From Grandma, she just gave it to me as a present." I replied with a hint of pride, which vanished as quickly as it came after her next words.

"Then go back to her and tell her to at least wash it because this smell is unbearable!"

I was unpleasantly surprised at first, but I soon realized that I did smell bad. The dress I received wasn't fresh. There was a smell of mustiness and something else in the air. I immediately went to Helena, took off the gift, and blurted out:

"I thought that if you give someone a gift, it should smell nice." I held out the dress to her. "Thank you, but I have to return it, this smell is terrible! Give me back the clothes I had on earlier."

"Are you kidding, you fool?" She looked at me with undisguised anger, leaving me stunned.

"Excuse me?"

"You ungrateful swine!"

After she hurled the insult, I quickly changed into the clothes I had left in the room earlier and went out, as after the initial shock, I didn't feel like listening to her derogatory remarks. Seeing that I wasn't particularly affected, she became even angrier, but I didn't hear if she said anything else. I headed toward other children to simply play. After a while, my father came and told me I was grounded.

"Dad, why? What did I do?"

"You always embarrass me," he mumbled under his breath.

"Is this about the dress? It stank, why was I supposed to accept it? You always tell me to speak the truth!"

I was confused, but I didn't get an answer to my questions. In his opinion, I did something that shouldn't have happened and for that, I was grounded for the entire weekend, watching TV and listening to my father's constant complaints. I tried to get lost in an old Polish TV series, but it was hard to concentrate because he was so persistent. In an angry mumble, he lectured me about my future:

"How could you be so ungrateful? You won't get anything more from Grandma. It's unthinkable for you to behave like that. What was that about?" I could feel his contemptuous gaze. "You won't amount to anything."

"Okay, I don't need anything, but why couldn't I tell Grandma the truth?"

I saw no understanding in my father's eyes, just disappointment and anger that became more frequent. He didn't say anything else and I lost myself in memories of my conversations with Helena.

Could my questions and honesty be so inappropriate? Was I supposed to believe her stories of wealth, when all I saw was a house that desperately needed renovation? I was just a child, a little child, and my questions about the lack of daily baths, the cheapest food, and things were treated as a complete lack of tact and manners. What kind of manners can you expect from a small child? I was curious, and her constant insults toward me were brushed off with laughter. Today, I know she wanted to control me because she couldn't stand that I didn't admire her.

Trying to mold a child to one's vision is very wrong. A child isn't our property, and we must understand this when bringing them into the world. They are an independent thinking person with their visions, moods, ideas, and character. We can help when they need it. We can provide needed role models, a sense of security, tenderness, love, understanding, and everything they can build from. We can show them the world and its possibilities, and help them deal with problems. But when we start forcibly pushing our way of thinking onto the child, reacting to their resistance in such a pathological way as Helena did, all we can expect is contempt. It's worth remembering that children perceive things differently than us, so the things we firmly force onto them will distort their views and their world which then has no chance of stability.

Damian

When a lie becomes the only solution

In theory, the truth is always the best answer. Sticking to the actual events, and avoiding sugar coating and deviations from reality allows for clear communication and a straightforward message. However, this is the case only when the environment is equally sincere and makes us feel safe. We feel valued and know that our words will be taken at face value. When a child finds himself in a stressful, even frightening situation, constructive thinking shuts down, and survival mode turns on. In such a state, a child cannot answer a question honestly because they're scared. But what happens when they're forced to?

I was nine when I was first accused of theft. My father didn't seek the truth; he believed what he heard from a stranger. He blamed me for the first time, and that was enough for my brother to build his shady future. When he noticed that no one believed me, he started taking things from the house.

I can't recall what he took first. I remember a bicycle, binoculars, a camera, and many other valuable items that my father began to miss. When it dawned on him that these things were not getting lost but disappearing forever, he gave us an ultimatum. He demanded that we confess.

He threatened to beat us until we admitted our guilt or lost consciousness. I remember my brother took a bike to a friend at that time. So, it wasn't a trivial thing anymore, like banknotes pulled from pants thrown into laundry. Yet, he kept silent. The threat of violence made me lie that I was the one taking things. That was the only lie I could muster then. When asked where all those things were, I was dumbfounded. I had no idea, and my brother still hadn't uttered a word. He was smirking. I felt he was playing with the situation, although maybe he was terrified and just seized the moment to avoid punishment. Was he more afraid of our father than I was?

I couldn't fathom the injustice and that he didn't do anything, seeing my suffering. Is that what a loving person does? Finally, the beating forced me to speak. I yelled out the made-up name of the person I supposedly sold the stolen items to, but he continued to hit me. He demanded an address, and we had to go there immediately. As we drove to the neighboring town, I desperately tried to find a way out but couldn't. In my desperation, I provided three addresses. Of course, at none of them did we find the girl who supposedly bought all the stolen items from me. I don't remember the weather, the houses we passed, or the time. I remember my father's fury and him asking passersby about someone they didn't recognize. When he returned to the car, frustrated and even angrier, I decided to tell him why I made it all up. For some reason, I confessed. I told him it wasn't me who stole, but Damian. I even told him where he could find those items because his son had taken them just two blocks away, within our housing complex.

I felt he believed me, but it was too complicated for him. He preferred to continue blaming and beating me. He didn't want and didn't need to look further. It would've taken too much of his time and energy.

I felt utterly helpless. The lack of understanding and complete distrust in my words made me doubt their value and truth. I started suspecting that I was naturally lying and began losing sight of what was a lie and what was the truth. This confusion blurred the line between reality and the distorted world image created by my toxic relationship with my father. Fear altered my thinking, reduced my concentration, and clouded my thoughts. For a child, this is severe. From that period, I mainly remember the confusion and my sore body aching almost daily.

This situation would repeat multiple times. All the money, all the alcohol, and all valuable items vanished, and so did my credibility. Each time, I was blamed, stuck in this cycle. My parents wanted to see me as guilty and never considered the possibility that their son could be the thief. Not even when others spotted the stolen items with him. They didn't believe the teachers who reported such incidents multiple times. They were always surprised and quickly forgot about it, dismissing it as a misunderstanding or trivial matter. They already had their culprit; they didn't need to look for others.

Punishments weren't limited to beating. They included house arrests lasting several days. For long days, I stayed indoors, while my brother roamed free, completely unobserved by our parents. Through the window, I heard and saw my friends playing. And I couldn't join them. Even now, the mere thought of it makes my stomach turn. I remember one evening during such an arrest. It was warm outside, and the kids were playing hide and seek and tag. Their joyous laughter echoed off the walls, and from despair, I dozed off. At some point, cheerful shouts woke me up. Right after that abrupt awakening, I felt an emptiness in my heart, wishing someone would take me away from this family, to a foster home or anywhere else.

Around that time, I began having suicidal thoughts and wishes to be kidnapped. When I was about five, I dreamt someone kidnapped me. Then, in that room, listening to the joy of other children, that dream came back and stayed with me. I vividly remembered every detail and emotion associated with it. I remembered the street I walked on, the silhouettes of the people in it, and the house I was heading toward. And I remember the paralyzing fear I felt upon waking up. How desperate was I that this dream became my rescue vision? I believed it would come true, dreaming about it wholeheartedly. And when it didn't, I fell deeper into my despair, completely losing my voice in this world. Such thoughts in a child signify extreme feelings, complete emotional abandonment, and loneliness that is simply unbearable.

Thinking about me as such a sad kid breaks my heart, and tears fill my eyes. Such heavy and intense experiences should never befall anyone, let alone a child.

One of the few lights in the darkness that began to envelop me was my Guardian Angel. In moments when it was truly bad, he would appear in the hallway. I would see a luminous figure, and I believed and knew that it was the only being capable of helping me. When I was scared, I thought of it, or him. When my father beat me, I believed he would have done so more harshly if my Guardian Angel hadn't come. Sometimes my father's hand hurt from the beating, and to me, that was a clear sign of help from this luminous being. It provided me with a point of reference and a tiny fraction of the safety I desperately needed.

At one point, I got so engrossed in lies about theft that I started stealing myself. I don't know if, in some dysfunctional way, I admired my brother, who so skillfully took everything from the house that could be sold. Unlike him, I didn't rob our parents but a store with cameras. The staff knew perfectly well what I was up to, but as long as I limited myself to candy bars and other small items, they did nothing. At some point, I became bolder and sneakily took things like an electric toothbrush. They couldn't ignore that, and at one point, they detained me and called the police. The officers took me to my father because I had to go to the police station with a guardian.

The police building wasn't particularly charming, and I wasn't entirely myself. I was terrified; my hands were shaking. Not because of the police but knowing my father would lay his hands on me again. After so many times, I hadn't gotten used to this fear. The tension in the air was palpable. Peeling, old, neglected walls, uncomfortable chairs, and silence while waiting for interrogation felt eternal. I didn't know if time was moving or if it had stubbornly stopped. Eventually, I was released and began the walk home. The prospect of family court wasn't scary at all.

My father ignored the passersby, kicking me openly, and angrily pulling my hair. I felt humiliated, anxiety growing as we got closer to home. Many people were around; we were walking through the estate. Yet no one intervened. No one questioned why an adult was roughing up a child. When we got home, it became clear to my parents. I had been responsible for all the thefts, and they saw no point in discussing it with me. I didn't need to speak. I was guilty, and another beating was due. That was, according to them, the best punishment and lesson for me. However, today I can't say if aggression toward me wasn't like a drug to them.

The day of the hearing came, and with all my naïveté, I believed someone would finally listen to me. That I could present everyone with my version of events. Full of hope and visions of a happy ending, I marched into court with a prepared speech. I was disappointed again. When I realized I was there only in principle and my fate had been decided without a chance for personal defense, I gave up. I remember something about a guardian and that there would be another hearing to check my progress or if I should be punished in a reformatory.

I don't remember when we were assigned a family guardian, but we were. He came to check on us for a while, but usually, only my mother was home. So it ended with just complaints about me, without physical abuse. At some point, a community officer was assigned to me. I wasn't attending school, so officially, he was supposed to take me. In practice, he came maybe once, and he had no authority over me.

There was an incident where fifty zlotys disappeared from my mother's purse. Of course, I was automatically to blame, so without resistance, I confessed again. I got called names and was beaten, but a few days later, the money was found. At the next hearing, my parents stated that I was making progress, and they had punished me last time for something I hadn't done. No one apologized. Life went on.

After that second hearing, when it became clear that I was truly innocent, something should have changed in my daily life, but it didn't. My father stopped beating me for a while, but that's because I learned to manipulate him slightly. To defend against the beating, I told him that kids were asking if my parents mistreated me because I was adopted. He calmed down for a while, but everything quickly returned to our daily norm. Unfortunately, no hearing changed anything in my life; it seemed to be another unpleasant event for them, not something worth reflecting on.

In a short time, I was caught again. This time it happened in a supermarket where for a while, my friends and I had been shoplifting candy. I can't fully remember what I felt when I was stealing those small things. Maybe it was a thrill or just a sense of belonging with the others who did it with me. But they could always share candy with one another; they were not afraid of punishment. I knew that I could get into trouble for even the smallest thing. But maybe this was my way of proving to myself that I could also belong somewhere, even if that place was among thieves.

They stole just for the act of stealing. The thrill, the free stuff, and the lack of responsibility. Or perhaps they didn't give it much thought. However, I stole because I wanted to eat candies that I simply didn't have at home. I didn't see anything wrong with it because I might not have realized how serious it was, especially since it was becoming a more frequent act. We were quite confident.

One day, on a whim, I did it alone. I remember being simply happy that I had something sweet in my pocket. I didn't feel guilty because I was too engrossed in the small pleasure I would feel in a moment. I got caught, and things escalated quickly. When I reached the checkout, security was already waiting for me. They quickly took me to the back room. I felt like my bladder wouldn't last. I was incredibly scared, tense, and paralyzed by fear. I wasn't thinking clearly, and when the guard asked who they should call, I said my father. They did, and I felt a burning sensation from the stress and the knowledge of what was about to happen. After calling my father, they also called the police.

"Why do you always have to be such a problem?" I heard from my father as we left the station. "Why are you such a nobody?" He yanked me around, a prelude to what awaited at home. I could see the emotions boiling in him. When he pushed me, he hissed: "Why do you steal? Why do you keep embarrassing me?"

I didn't respond. When we got home, he quickly got down to business, hitting me all over. Again. But this time he finished quickly, and I could go to sleep.

I also remember discussing this with my mother because her attitude then was very hurtful. She didn't hit me, but she gave me the feeling that I was genuinely a bad person. After the police told me I would likely get community service for all this, I asked my mother for her opinion. I remember that only I was to be punished because I was the only one caught in the act.

"Mom, what do you think about me getting punished and all of them not?"

"What are you looking for now, someone to blame?" she snapped back, displeased.

"But others were stealing earlier too..."

"...and so? The important thing is you're getting punished, why look for others?"

"But if we all stole, shouldn't we all be punished, don't you think that would be fair?"

Silence.

"Is it more important that I get punished, or that we all get punished fairly?"

I never got an answer. I probably just walked away during the conversation, knowing I would neither receive a response nor reach a constructive conclusion. I felt it was easier for her to defend other kids, while just punishing her own without questioning. In her eyes, I deserved the punishment, and the others didn't need to be held accountable because why bother? After all, I was the one who got caught, so what's the point in looking for other culprits?

Wouldn't it be better if they had sat down with me and explained the consequences, asked me why I did it and tried to understand a growing child? Is this truly how one should raise a child? Pointing out their mistakes and dictating how things should be done? Is punishment for the sake of punishment the best educational and comfortable approach for everyone involved? I understand that consequences are often important, but there's a better way. Instilling understanding of the situation in a child and trying to understand their reasons. Communication, empathy, and direct conversation. These are the foundations of upbringing, something my parents had no clue about.

When beating is not the biggest problem anymore

Physical pain related to being hit is a shock for a child's body, whether they expect the beating or not. At that moment, the body suffers, and the mind tries to focus on finding an explanation or something to alleviate the pain. Recovery from such pain does not end when the bruises and blood stains fade away. It all stays in the body and the mind for much longer, or even forever. Sometimes a lack of understanding, a sudden feeling, or a state induced by a certain incident makes us detach from the body to cease to feel or to feel less. To only observe what is happening and avoid being a part of it. Today I know that the moment in which you can see your own body lying on the floor is called an out-of-body experience. It usually happens to people suddenly, or in critical moments, when they detach themselves mentally because of the shock they are going through. Yet it wasn't my father beating me that made me experience that.

I learned very early what it means to feel such detachment from oneself. I was eleven. My mind could not take the sight of my brother masturbating over me. I remember that he did this to me when I was ill. I was sleeping, exhausted due to food poisoning, while my parents went with my younger sister to visit some friends. I thought that I was safe, if only for that moment, and I let my guard down. I woke up suddenly as someone was dragging me by my ankles across the floor, taking no notice of furniture or thresholds.

I quickly realized what he was doing, and at the same time, I was detached from myself, observing him taking off my t-shirt without ceremony, as he couldn't resist his sick desire.

"It's so arousing," he whispered feverishly, "I'm gonna cum on your cleavage."

I was petrified, and because of that, I couldn't move. When I felt a guck on my breasts, my soul came back to my body. I was utterly struck by the disgusting smell, while my brother was saying something. In a sub-

61

conscious rather than conscious way, I understood that I was to wash my-self and get cleaned up fast because our parents would be back soon. I went to the bathroom, to wash away not only the smell but also what just happened. I couldn't or maybe I didn't want to realize that I was a victim of sexual harassment. I cried out of helplessness for a few hours, being unable to get out of the bathroom. Curled up on the floor, I was trying to find something to hold onto so that I could feel that it was just a dream. But it was crystal clear that it was a cruel twist of fate. I wanted to wake up, but reality would burst into my consciousness, hurting my soul and marking it for the rest of my life. It was only when my father screamed at me to get out that I did so, without looking at him. That day the bathroom became the place where I would seek refuge.

Unfortunately, it wasn't a single incident, but the beginning of a traumatic time, when every moment spent with my father could end up with me ha-ving a new bruise and experiencing physical pain, and every moment wi-thout him or my mother resulted in mental pain and aversion to life. My brother knew he could get away with that because he quickly realized that I wasn't going to tell anybody. I felt helpless as I had no one to turn to. For a very long time, I suppressed those incidents, and when I had moments of comprehending them, I told myself that everyone would just think that it was my fault, not my brother's. I didn't want to make it worse, I stagna-ted, wanting only to survive mentally and live on. At that time I felt rela-tively safe when my mother was home. It didn't protect me from my vio-lent father, but it kept my disturbed brother away from me. When my mo-ther started to do outwork, I desperately held onto that, because it meant that for most of the day, someone would be home. Yet it was just another way to dim my fear, which came back double-barreled when my mother had to leave the house to go to work.

I was in my room with my two-year-old sister, who at that time was the only reason for me to smile if only for a moment. I foresightedly loc-ked the top lock of the apartment doors and I indulged in innocent play. Yet I still couldn't let my ever-vigilant guard down, and I felt a strange knot in my chest. I was right about my hunch; constantly watching the door, I finally heard the sound I was afraid of. When the intercom buzzed, I had no doubts that it was my brother trying to get inside. I didn't react, but my fear increased. I tried to ignore it and focus on playing with my sister, yet soon I heard footsteps on the staircase and my neighbor's voice, who probably passed my brother by in the hallway. I desperately held onto the fact that I had closed the door, yet unfortunately a few seconds later it was clear that it provided no protection and there was no place for me to feel safe.

First, he pulled the door handle, and when the door didn't open, he tried again. I froze and I couldn't breathe. Then I heard a crash and saw the door coming off the hinges. Instinctively, I picked up my sister and screaming out of fear, I tried to flee the apartment. Of course, he grabbed me, ignoring my panicking, although today I could swear that each time it gave him extra motivation to commit that crime. My little sister was not an obstacle for him, and I was still holding her in my arms. Without saying a word he dragged me to a room where he would usually struggle with me and my clothes, and in an instant I started to tussle double-barreled, as I was also thinking about the child next to me. We were both screaming, yet only I knew what was going to ensue. When he ripped off my bra and my t-shirt, my sister tried to put the clothes on me with her clumsy little hands, yet my brother brutally pushed her away. I will never forget the sight of my sister sitting down, watching that repelling scene with her eyes wide open, full of fear and unable to understand what was happening.

At that moment I ceased to fight and I just wanted him to finish as quickly as possible. So that I could hug my sister and soothe her fear, as I couldn't do the same with mine. When he finished, I went to wash myself, simultaneously suppressing the real meaning of that situation. I couldn't term it, so my only option was to loathe myself and fear my brother. I didn't utter a word for the next couple of hours even though I was spending time playing with my sister. I wanted to survive and not show her my pain, but I was also just a child and I wasn't very good at hiding my emotional state. I felt like an animal, chased into the corner from all sides.

I couldn't understand why absolutely no one was interested in me. Why didn't my own mother, entering the house through the broken door, care about the story behind it? Why didn't she ask me the question I so desperately needed to release my pent-up emotions? To explain that it wasn't my fault? Why was I only given to hear that I shouldn't do it anymore? The dull feeling in my chest was slowly but surely spreading throughout my body, creating a numbness that wouldn't leave me for years. The walls aren't made of paper, but didn't the neighbors hear my screams? My crying? And the doors being kicked out of the frame? Their ignorance and lack of empathy strike my adult self. The older neighbors were sitting in their armchairs and on their sofas, probably drinking tea and getting annoyed by the sounds disturbing their peace. And those playing with their beloved children outside didn't pay any attention to the constant quarrels that, after all, had nothing to do with them. Loneliness was my daily reality. It invaded my soul, gradually losing the way out.

Perhaps things are different now and people respond to the suffering of others. On the Internet, you can find hundreds of fundraisers for sick children, thousands of articles about supporting the poorest, texts that raise awareness about orphanages, and foundations for those who are mentally or genetically ill. But do we know how to react here and now? Any support for others is good, but sometimes that first second counts, the moment of our reaction, which should happen when we see someone being wronged. When you see a child being kicked by an adult on the street, when a crying, lonely boy walks by, or someone lies breathless. These are just moments in these people's lives, which could change so much if someone passing by would just be human. I don't know the feeling of support from childhood. No one was able to help me. And probably no one felt the need to.

When memories fade, but don't disappear

We tend to idealize the past. Maybe the human mind doesn't like to store the worst of memories, but it also can't get rid of them. In any case, it is often difficult to recall the worst moments. Or maybe it is a way to keep calm? Or keep one's sanity? One can often hear about situations when victims suppress the details of their traumatic experiences.

Most of the incidents when my brother hurt me are blurry in my memory. I think that the only explanation is that my mind tries to squelch my traumatic memories so that they don't color the present. It is not normal to suppress something like that. I'm trying to recollect as much as I can to write down the memories and to give vent to the emotions that are still in me.

The first time he came on my breasts, but after that he went further. At the mere thought of that, I have a lump in my throat and I feel sick. One time he took off my pants and my underwear and while touching my private parts he told me he would lick me out. I was paralyzed after hearing these words and I remember that I just desperately wanted him not to do it. I couldn't defend myself and I didn't know how to, because fear deprived me of any tools. He didn't do it eventually, but I think he enjoyed the mere planning of what he could do to me.

Each subsequent time was worse because I expected he would do what he said he would. The strain of expecting him to carry out his threats and the final relief when he didn't carry out some of them were crushing. One time, when he was doing it to me I was screaming; I don't remember why but I was screaming very loud. He told me to be quiet or he would hurt me. And I was quiet because I was scared. It had happened multiple times by the time I told my mother.

It got to the point where from one time to the next I felt an unpleasant strain. The tension grew until he used me again, and then there was temporary relief that I was safe. It lasted for such a short time that it could not grant me the piece I needed so badly.

After one of the incidents, I don't remember whether it was significant or not, there was to be a school dance. I was in the first year of middle school and I went to it to just dance. For the most part, I had a lot of fun, but at one point I realized what happened before the school dance, and I stood against the wall. The music and other people's voices completely faded away, I lost track of time and space, and in my mind, I could see the exact image of what happened before. I saw, second after second, what my brother was doing to me and I could not control those images. I could only watch and painfully go through it once again. I woke up from this when a couple of people approached me. At first, I wanted to tell them everything, but then I didn't know how to put it into words. How to tell someone that your brother treats you like that?

I remember that in middle school I attended dance class. One day my friends were supposed to meet me at my house and we would go together. They came a little early and my brother was sleeping. I was really afraid that they would wake him up so I asked them to be quiet. I swear that I worried that their presence wouldn't stop him from hurting me again. I was afraid they would be witnesses to that, and as a consequence, everyone would find out. I experienced a significant inner conflict that didn't allow me to make a rational judgment of that situation. I worried that everyone would talk about it; I wanted someone to find out and at the same time, I didn't want anyone to know. I would tell my mother what my brother was doing to me, yet I was afraid to tell anyone else. Maybe I didn't expect any help, only being invidiously labeled? That I will be a hot gossip for people dying to hear some sick sensation? I was an extremely lost and hurt child and I felt such a relief when we left the apartment that my friends easily noticed it and asked me what was wrong. They tried to find out why I was so scared of my brother. They could see on multiple occasions how strange he could behave, so they had to guess if only a little that my fear was reasonable and real. I only said that I didn't want to provoke him into another argument and that it was best for everyone to stay quiet in such a situation.

One time he came home. I was in my room, I think I was doing homework. It was warm outside and the window in the room was open. There were a lot of kids on the playground. He lifted me out of the chair and I started to scream right away. He let me go and went over to the window. I had a few seconds to run away, but paralyzing fear overcame me and I couldn't move. I was just standing there. That window reminds me of one more incident. My father was beating me because he had a few zlotys in his pocket and then they were gone. I remember the pattern of similar situations. My father would put his pants with money in the pockets on the washing machine, my brother would take the money and then I was to be blamed and no one believed me that I had nothing to do with that. Coming back to the window. My father was beating me, and I cried very loud, shouting at him to stop. Then he went over to the window and closed it telling me to be quiet. I said that in that case, he had to stop beating me because it hurt and I would scream. Then he started to beat me so hard and with such ferocity, with such an expression on his face, that I stopped asking him and waited for him to finish. I felt like a rag doll, or like a punching bag. I thought it was better to be quiet because then it all would be over soon.

Being sexually abused by my brother and being beaten by my father was strongly connected in my head. In both cases, I was paralyzed by fear and I would stop screaming after they threatened me. At one point I also stopped crying, anonymously holding back my reactions. I couldn't run away because my body wouldn't listen to me. I waited for them to finish.

Those experiences caused me to stop talking about my feelings with anyone for many years. I closed myself off to sincere relationships thinking it to be a natural course of things. For a long time, I felt that I couldn't and shouldn't talk about how I felt, what I was afraid of, and what I wanted and needed. I was consumed by the traumatic experiences that would drag me down every day. A genuine smile regarding the members of my family was long gone, and I began to believe that I didn't deserve a different life. Yet I was doing it subconsciously. I knew it was all wrong, and I rebelled, but when it came down to it, I was quiet out of fear and lack of understanding. Over time, I stopped talking, screaming, and revolting. I would endure pain in silence thinking it would hurt least, and I wouldn't provoke them

into another degenerate behavior and they wouldn't cause me more pain than usual.

Coming to terms with one's fate is often a symptom of complete helplessness regarding hurtful incidents and thoughts coming to your head. Pain in the whole body is a symptom of fear, grief, or other strong feelings that come in harmful situations. Being paralyzed and being unable to utter a single word may be a defense mechanism, which activates in moments of increased stress. It seems to be the same in the case of hiding the most painful memories in your head. How can it help a child, though, who gets to know daily life by experiencing everyday wrongdoings?

When the pattern isn't what it should be

When mom and dad are not our anchor during childhood, we don't have any fundamental stability to hold onto. A little child's sense of security lacks a foundation through which they could gain strength and confidence. Existing in the vacuum of insecurity and constant lack of understanding, it is not possible to develop a sense of such important values as self-love. One person who would care, who would soothe loneliness could fix it all.

The pain settled down in my heart. It wasn't piercing and unexpected. It was pervasive. Apathy was sometimes replaced by stress and anxiety, and sometimes by grief over something that I never really had. I remembered my childhood and the way my parents treated me. Maybe there was love somewhere back then, but I think a cumbrous one, or difficult for me to recall. I remember that my brother was always interested in me in a sick way. One time he took me to the bathroom and told me to watch him pee. He didn't do it in secret, my parents were home and I was only a couple of years old. Their reaction wasn't right. They made some jokes, laughed about the situation and probably decided not to speak about it again because they never did.

Wasn't it the right moment to analyze my brother's inappropriate behavior? Shouldn't they have stepped up and explained to him that it was wrong and that you can't force anyone to see your private parts? Maybe he was already disturbed and they could have helped him so that he wouldn't hurt anyone in the future. Maybe it was only then that he felt that what he did was natural and harmless. Unfortunately, they were only present physically in our lives, providing no real care or support, which may lead to the conclusion that not everyone should have children.

After my brother proved that the front door was no obstacle for him to get in, I came up with another way to provide myself with some sense of security and some time needed to run away in a pinch. I noticed that when I open the bathroom door and I hook them to the handle of the front door, there is a chance they would open yet not enough for someone to get into the apartment. When I was home alone, being aware of that calmed me down if only a little. During the week, when my brother was in the dorm in his special needs school, the level of my anxiety was lower, yet fear had become my everyday companion, which constantly dragged me down. Still, no one paid any attention to me.

It was Friday, and due to increasing anxiety that caused me to feel a knot in my chest, I couldn't focus on any of the classes. I didn't want to come home, because I was simply scared.

That feeling wasn't just a slight dislike. It was palpable, heavy and sticky. Opening the door I heard my mother's voice and anxiety vanished for a moment, letting in the joy that I didn't have to be afraid for a while. My brother came home indeed, yet we only ate dinner together, without touching on any sensitive topics. After the meal, my family decided to go out but I didn't want to. I decided to stay and have some rest after that emotional strain that I had been experiencing all day. I wanted to be alone and let go of my fear for a moment. I slammed the door, lay down on my bed, and closed my eyes. I had no time to let go and fall asleep, as after thirty minutes I heard his footsteps again. I believed that my method with the bathroom door would work, yet it was of no obstacle to him. He walked across my flimsy means of protection, trampling it completely, while

I curled up on the bed, crossing in my head the limits of fear and not knowing how far they could be pushed. I didn't move as I wasn't able to. My body was paralyzed and I couldn't breathe, and I could not defend myself this time. I didn't struggle, I tried to hold back disgust. I felt sick and then, passively waiting for the turn of events, I threw up. He didn't care, it didn't impact his pathological fury. After he finished I was only able to get up and take my stained body to the bathroom, where I broke down further. I don't know how long I was there, but suddenly I heard my mother's voice, and she brought someone over.

I slowly opened the door and heard my aunt asking what happened, whether I was fine and why I threw up. At that moment I wanted to tell her. Quickly, clearly, and without beating around the bush. I felt confident about what I wanted to do and I opened my mouth, but when I looked over at my mother my confidence vanished. It was pointless. My hope faded away and I just told her that I had a stomach ache. I cleaned up the floor and went to my room. No one inquired whether I told the truth. No one noticed the yawning emptiness in my eyes.

How resigned a child must be to not want to ask for help? What lesson do their parents want to teach them by constantly disappointing them, which should not be a part of a child's experience?

There was one incident where I could see with my own eyes what my brother was capable of. I remember that I was about six years old. There were two lakes around the area, a castle, a beach, and a long boardwalk. I would often go for a walk with my friends by one of the lakes or walk a dog. That lake was frozen at that time. We would often walk across it. That day I saw my brother banging little kittens' heads against the ice. Another day he again held some small animals in his hands and banged their heads against an old metal dumpster. Everyone knew about this. They talked about it at school, when I first saw it I think I told my parents about what he did. It would recur, but not only this. Allegedly he would grab little girls in the park and tell them to take off their underwear to look what was underneath it. He attempted to set the school on fire and he did many other abnormal things. He would beat children at school, and he would scream like a monkey during recess.

My parents knew about that and it never occurred to them to take him to a psychologist and help him. Maybe then he would have a chance to live without hurting others and himself. Yet anything he did could not catch the attention of my parents. It is incomprehensible and terrifying and that is how I feel about it to this day. At one point he went to juvie, then to a school for a short period and finally, my parents put him into a special needs school in Malbork, where he was five days a week. This situation was overwhelming for my father, as he couldn't stand the fact that his son didn't function properly. He took out all of his anger, disappointment, and grief on my mother, faulting her for putting him there for five days because she didn't want to take care of him. He told her that he had neglected him, that she hadn't guided him properly. He was violent and unfair, even when he was right about some of it. Yet ironically it was he who was never around, he found a job in Germany and I dare to say that the salary wasn't the main incentive, but the possibility to make only my mother responsible for their children. It was comfortable for him. After all, he could have taken us to Germany and maybe it would have been easier for him. Of course, my mother also reproached him but she was mostly at the receiving end of faulting anyway. It was wrong that she worked, that she stayed at home, that she took care of us wasting time and that she didn't take care of us enough. That she cooked and she didn't, everything was wrong.

Such scenes were an inherent part of my childhood, so it is difficult to expect that any of us, the children, could have been developing properly. Each of us had our share of problems and disturbances, with which we had to deal as best as we could.

When a night lamp becomes a necessity

It often happens that children can't fall asleep in pitch darkness. Maybe they don't feel fully safe, maybe they need the light in case of a bad dream.

It's much worse when they hope to find relief and safety in this light, and when it goes out, they feel overcome with panic that someone is watching them.

Even today, when I'm an adult and I'm safe, I often need this night lamp, because at some moments I feel anxious again that someone's eyes are looking at my body with bad intentions and sick images because such an experience was always part of my life. When I write that I go to my room, I mean a room that could be shared by everyone. There were no locks on the doors, and the possibility of having a soothing rest alone was very rare. I didn't have a moment of privacy even while taking a shower. When I realized that someone was watching me through the gable vent in the doors, I felt squeamish and since then I would put the laundry basket by the door when I took off my clothes so that I could have at least a minimum of privacy.

I also remember how Damian tried to take out a small hatch in the bathroom door when I took a shower, telling me to get out and clean after the dog. I told him that I wouldn't do it and he could do it as well as it was his dog too. And that if he tried to touch the window I would scream so loud that everyone would hear and the police would come. Because I knew what he was trying to do to me. He let it go and told me that he would catch me later.

Looking back, I think that he must have felt he deserved it. I still can't understand how my parents could have played it down.

When it seemed that there was no way out regarding my situation, it turned out that it could be worse. My mother told me one day that she had undertaken nightwork. It was another blow because I hadn't realized that I could feel even less safe at home. My mind was racing because I had nowhere to hide, I wouldn't be able to defend myself when I was asleep, and the bathroom was not a good enough cover. Unfortunately, I quickly realized that I was right about worrying about that. The first night, I fell asleep with my sister next to me in bed. As I was tired, I didn't think about hiding and just dozed off. I woke up due to a pain in my body and a concurrent, strange, very unpleasant feeling. I was so bewildered I couldn't think about what was happening and when I opened my eyes I saw my brother's friends over me. I quickly realized that a few more people were standing by the bed, including my brother. I managed to spring out of bed and call the police. The people present were under the influence of marijuana, which could be discerned because of the smell and their uncontrollable laughter. They didn't take the phone away from me but instead tried to calm the police by saying things like:

"Officer, there's nothing wrong, everything's fine!"

For a couple of minutes, I couldn't explain in a clear way what had happened and the officer didn't understand why I couldn't deal with the problem myself. Finally, a police officer was sent to our house and he told everyone to leave. Once again I didn't get support from anyone, and when my mother came home, tired and offended, I couldn't tell her what had happened. I didn't want to hear that she didn't believe me, I didn't have the energy for that.

A child called the police, asked for help and told them the situation. An officer shouldn't, can't undermine a child's fear and helplessness, doubting their ability to defend themselves. Since I reached out for help, and in consequence, I felt humiliated, did I have a chance to feel safe? That man saved the situation in a way, telling the unwelcome guests to leave, yet earlier it was implied that I was overreacting and should deal with that on my own. A little girl harassed by a couple of boys should be able to kick them out of the house on her own?

When no one wants to understand

Telling someone about one's problems should be natural. The chance to share what hurts us and raises our doubts is equally important in adulthood. The bond with one's partner and their ability to understand and make one feel safe give a huge sense of support and a chance to build a valuable relationship. When a child tries to express their emotions and tell their mom or dad what caused them pain, they naturally expect understanding, support, and love. When in exchange for their honesty a child receives a lack of understanding, and their problem is ignored, they stop believing in their self-worth and their value.

I was eleven years old and I remember that Damian had sexually abused me a couple of times. The moment came when the accumulation of such incidents caused me to muster the courage. Or maybe it's too strong a word for desperately trying to find the way out of this situation. I felt a little more confident thanks to my friend sitting next to me. As I was sitting opposite my mother, I gave vent to my feelings as it seemed to be the only moment when I could put them in words, presenting the whole truth about what was going on in her own house. My body and my voice were shaking, and the knot in my stomach was in charge of nausea caused by anxiety. I wanted to feel some relief, I wanted to hear that my fear was over, yet I felt disbelief and shock instead.

My mother started laughing at me. I couldn't understand what had just happened, and when I heard her laughter turning slowly into silence I waited to hear what she had to say. All I heard was:

"Stop, just stop. I wonder what else you'll come up with so that no one thinks about how stupid you are. Get hold of yourself and improve your math grades."

She said that I could have come up with a much better excuse. It made me unable to utter a word for the next two days. My head couldn't contain the chaotic thoughts that tried to understand why my mother didn't believe that I was suffering. Why was it so easy for her to just see it as a teenage girl's made-up story? Could it have worked at all? Throughout my childhood, I was a punching bag for my family. Literally and figuratively. Making fun of me was natural for them. Humiliating me was their daily activity, and tormenting me ineffable pleasure. They saw it as jokes that lifted their mood, ignoring how damaging it was for me. Did they have bad in-

tentions?

For the next twenty years, I didn't find an answer to my desperate question and with each day I felt inferior to others. It was only when I was in therapy that I realized why my mother had reacted in such a way.

However, this couldn't erase the twenty years of loneliness and lack of understanding and support from my family. At that time I carried an unimaginable burden every day. The pain worsened when I saw or felt that my friends were loved by their parents, and they were beaming with that love. That good family relations could exist, as well as bonds and healthy closeness. That one could like coming home. That the bed could be associated with warmth. That others could be listened to and understood. Why was I deprived of that? Why did I experience only humiliation, dislike, and a complete lack of trust? At that time I couldn't be sure of anything. I could be beaten for getting out of bed too early, and every moment of being home alone could entail my brother's disgusting behavior.

Today I know that a complete lack of empathy and a lack of consideration for others' feelings should be punished. They were back then. And I suffered severely. I had no shield that could defend me from others' words and actions, that's why I couldn't believe I was worth anything. My sense of self-worth was non-existent, and my hell lasted until I was seventeen years old. However, that wasn't the definitive end of it.

A person rejected by those around him or her feels awful. Hardly anyone can deal with the fact that no one treats them seriously, doesn't listen to them and ignores their every word. In the case of a child, the effect is devastating. Growing up lonely is one thing, but walking on hot coals and the constant risk of getting hit can be destructive.

When your pain doesn't matter

It's important to remember that what we see in others on a daily basis may have nothing to do with their everyday reality. It's very easy to create an image of a perfect family with what you tell others, or with artificial, occasional behavior. Going to church just because it's expected, having polite conversations with others where only safe topics are addressed, or showing affection to your children only for show. All of this can be called a smoke screen of reality. Or perhaps it's fear of realizing that one is simply not living the way they should.

Interestingly, my family was religious in some way, although it really had nothing to do with true life according to Catholic traditions. Aside from devotions at the cross in the countryside, aside from praying the rosary and weekly church visits by my father's mother, or her sporadic pilgrimages, there was little evidence that they knew who this God was. I remember at the age of twelve or thirteen, I decided to cut myself. I did it very clumsily and ineffectively because I simply didn't know how to go about it. Did anyone at that time, with all that artificial piety, at least pray for me? Not necessarily. My brother, as soon as he saw what had happened, began to mock me. Because it was another proof for him that I was a life's loser. My parents didn't pay any attention at all, or if they did, it was indifferent to them because they simply didn't comment on it at all. What was clear was an awkward, heavy silence.

My brother, as usual wanting to draw attention to himself, said what I had done when our cousin was visiting us. He did it in an original way, as he told my cousin that she wasn't so hip because her hands were smooth, not cut up. He achieved the desired effect because my father was visibly shocked and my mother loudly exhaled. Some time later they talked to him. The conversation, however, was not about the risk of their daughter's dying, but the inappropriateness of raising such a topic at the table.

It was yet another proof that I didn't mean anything to them. I didn't ne-

cessarily expect some human reactions on their part because to me they were still incapable of having more complex emotions. Unfortunately, despite all that I still felt pain and permanent rejection.

I have to say that I didn't feel like a human being in my family house. I was much closer to being a thing that they could spit on at any moment, and move, destroy, abuse or just ignore. No one there cared about me. In front of other people, they acted like concerned parents when in reality they made my life hell. It all ended when I met Tomek, so despite his negative impact on me I continued to be with him. Because he gave me some semblance of freedom. A moment of breath. My father stopped beating me, and Damian stopped sexually abusing me.

Agata

When you become a mother while still a child

You can often encounter a pathological situation where parents shift the responsibilities of caring for an infant onto an older child. It may seem helpful and sweet, and hugely supportive, but it's not. A parent is responsible for their children, and if they do not understand this, they should not have children. By entrusting an infant to the care of another child of theirs, they rob them of their childhood under the guise of support. It's cruel because the love for the infant blinds the child to the world. It breeds guilt in them for feeling tired, a sense of insignificance because their time is not important, loneliness because help is not coming from anywhere. And sometimes even hatred for the little one. How difficult is it for a young mother to raise a small child? So how traumatic must it be for a child?

I was ten years old when my sister Agata was born, and I remember how quickly my parents transferred the responsibility of caring for her onto me. Mother went back to work, I think to Biedronka supermarket. Father didn't pay attention to the situation at all. No one talked to me about it. She simply got a job, informed me about it, and that was the end of the topic. I had to give up all extracurricular activities, such as the dance classes that I loved, theater classes, time at the daycare center, or any outings with friends.

I remember wanting to go out on rollerblades, which lay in the basement, and my mother asked me how I intended to ride rollerblades while pushing a stroller. I then replied that I wanted to go rollerblading and that I didn't have to take Agatka. There was no discussion because my needs didn't count. Here I'm reminded of my mother's clean clothes and leather boots in contrast to my dirty school attire and worn-out clothes.

In the hours when they were not there, and even in many others, I became the mother of an infant who was my sister, not my child. It seemed that for my parents, the matter was closed. They were not there, so I had to take care of the child. For me, despite the confusion and tremendous stress associated with it, it was obvious that I had to do it. But it was too much. I remember that the care so deeply ingrained itself in my daily life that I took Agatka everywhere. To every date. My first kiss looked like this: with one hand I held the stroller, gently rocking it, and with the other, I embraced the boy when he decided to kiss me. I took her to every tea, hot chocolate, or other outing with friends. I had to pick her up from kindergarten, and later also take her there.

Once, when Agatka was about two years old and her daytime naps had become somewhat more regular, I decided to take the opportunity. During one of them, I ran out of the apartment to bring something to a friend who lived two blocks away. On the way, I remembered that I hadn't locked the terrace, and we lived on the first floor. So from the window, from my friend's apartment, I watched that terrace almost continuously. I remember turning away for a moment when I reached for the tea. When my gaze returned to the terrace, Agatka was already standing on the railing. I froze, but luckily only for a few terrifying seconds. After a moment I began to act. I ran out of the apartment and rushed toward the house, simultaneously screaming at Agatka to come down immediately. Fortunately, she understood and quickly directed her little legs back home. I rushed into the apartment and grabbed her, luckily nothing had happened. I managed to put her back to sleep, but after that, I never left.

It was only then that I understood that I couldn't leave her alone. I couldn't anticipate such situations because I was a child and no one talked to me about how to take care of a toddler.

During her naps, I started reading books, resting, and doing anything I could do at home. I was very affected by the situation, and the realization that I probably should tell my parents about it didn't help to reduce my stress. I didn't know if I would again be the guilty, thoughtless, and bad one, or if perhaps my situation would slightly improve and my time for friends, walks, or just some elements of childhood would return instead of the care that an adult should provide. I decided to take a risk and tell them what happened. I told them, but I didn't get the response I was hoping for.

Of course, all the blame for what happened, for the fact that they had a third child without realizing that they didn't have time for it, fell on me. I remember looking at them with pity, recalling the basics of protected sex, which I was currently learning in family life education classes. The epithets that I had to listen to were partly hurting me and partly stopped in the thicket of my regret and doubt in the maturity of the people who used them. Their impetuousness and confidence, assurances of my responsibility, and how bad and useless I was, were unimaginable.

I was twelve years old, for heaven's sake. It was one of those first moments when I thought that my parents were mentally amoebas. They told me then that their childhood was many times worse than mine, that they had it tough, that I had nothing to complain about, that I had food to eat, and so on. However, when I boldly suggested to them that if that was the case, why were they serving me the same? Did they want my childhood to be just as hard, or were they trying to compensate for something else? Of course, this was an insult to their majesty accompanied by a flowery indignation and a speech including parts about how I dared to say such a thing to them.

It was a vicious cycle. Taking care of Agata, I didn't have time to do my homework properly, let alone review the material or any study. I didn't have the time or the opportunity. I couldn't focus on it because I was also tired both mentally and physically. And they expected me to have the best possible grades, and to come home with an excellent report card. Of course, they poured out their grievances and anger on me when this didn't happen, still not understanding that it was all their fault. Their inept parenting, lack of imagination, complete absence of empathy, and basic knowledge regarding safe sex at a theoretically mature age. In practice, only physically. They were even surprised by notes in the student record about the lack of a uniform, art supplies, and many other things they considered unnecessary. They believed they didn't have money for that. I was responsible for my remarks and grades. Just as I was responsible for myself and my little sister.

Marzena

When you don't have a mom, just a mother

A mom is the first person in the world that a child loves unconditionally. It's to her that they reach out with requests for food, affection, comfort, and support. It's in her arms that they seek solace while crying. It's with her that they create the first, true, deep bond. Over time, this bond transforms into a looser, more flaccid thread, but there's still a place for that first, unconditional love. However, when a mother doesn't want to or can't nurture this, the child also doesn't learn to. They simply accept it as a natural fact that they have something of an obligation to their mother.

My mother wasn't pleased with the fact that we came into the world at all. But it happened. That's probably why, since life didn't go her way, she became such an unhappy, frustrated woman. Looking at her young pictures, I see a smiling girl with a radiant gaze. Curly, dark blonde hair, smooth skin, and peace mixed with joy. I wasn't able to capture that in reality, during the many years I lived with her under one roof.

If I had to compare her with my father, she was a better parent. I remember she took me and my siblings to various extracurricular activities. To art and dance. I even remember one moment when she stood up for me. At one of the first singing lessons, I performed a song by the famous singer Anna. I knew the text well because learning by heart was never a big problem for me. I could quickly take things in, especially those that interested me. Anyway, in this case, it wasn't everything I needed to sing the song correctly. I did it just off-key and I heard from the teacher that if I intended to sing like that, I might as well not come to the next lessons. It wasn't pleasant, so I told my mother about the situation right after the classes. She entered the room and, while always behaving tactfully and gently, asked what the matter was. I remember she quickly dispelled such comments from the teacher by stating that it was her job to bring out my voice and it depended on her whether she could straighten me out in this regard. It's hard to expect a child at the second music lesson to sing perfectly in tune and without mistakes, after all, that's irrational. Why then would they come to lessons? I never heard that kind of snide remark again, and those singing lessons went on in their way. That was one of those moments when I felt my mom's support. I haven't forgotten it because there were few of them.

The second such situation was after a fight, or some scuffle with kids in the neighborhood. She must have heard about it because when I came home she asked me if she should go to those kids and talk to them. I didn't want that, so she agreed with my decision and didn't bring it up again. I don't know if it was more convenient for her or if she simply respected my request.

In my opinion, she has an artistic soul and is very creative and open to such things. What impressed me was that when we were little, she left us with a nanny so she could go to work. My father blamed her for this because everything she earned went to pay the nanny's salary. However, no one looked at the fact that, by doing this, she was gaining experience and earning her retirement. It also allowed her to have contact with people, to develop, and to live at least to some extent as she wanted. For me, this simply means that not every job has to be just a source of money for someone.

It was and remains unimaginable to me. Even a friend whose dad was in jail received more care, love, and attention than I did. She would come home to a clean house, have a warm meal waiting, and she felt the support from her mother. She would ask her how school was, about the new boyfriend, about her friends. But today I feel resentment; back then, I was simply surprised that parents could show such interest in their children. They were poor, but it was with them that I first saw what a family could look like from the emotional side. It was a huge discovery and breakthrough, allowing me to believe that my father was wrong when he said that I shouldn't associate with them because they were the ultimate pathology and people who did not live correctly.

I remember the verbal skirmishes, perpetual dissatisfaction, constant complaints about the lack of money, complete ignorance, and the sadness I felt in my relationship with her. As a child, I made many natural attempts to establish some connection but I never managed to trust her. Perhaps her emotional unavailability contributed to this, or perhaps her childhood problems as well. Regardless of the reasons, she mainly offered me criticism, aggression, and passivity, while others hurt me right under her nose. She never wanted to believe my versions of events, which she could laugh off. It was easier for her to believe that her daughter had done something wrong and should be punished. Those few moments when she was younger when she wanted to support me in some way and help me are so fleeting in my memory that I feel she did it out of obligation. Not out of love.

I remember a situation that clearly shows me today the attitude she had toward me. At my school, collections of clothes and necessary items for the poorest children were organized from time to time. Although we needed it, we were not considered because my father worked in Germany. I then had an idea related to the fact that my brother and I went to different schools. I thought it would be nice to organize such a clothing collection at his school. So I wrote a letter to the teacher. I tried very hard to make my writing as straight as possible, and since my style to this day is quite loose, it was a big challenge. A several times rewritten and well-thought-out official letter, with which I had high hopes. I included a message that we organize such collections at our school and asked if she would like to do the same. I noted that it would be a collection for specific children we know and who live in an orphanage. When I finished, my mother's friend was over, and I came in with the note, laid it in a visible place, and explained to my mother what it was about. My brother was at home at the time and happened to walk by.

She took the letter from me. It was carefully packed in a white envelope, and she tore it up saying that I wasn't going to write any little notes, let alone send them. That's what my initiatives looked like. Any of them. It's easy to guess how quickly I lost enthusiasm and heart for them.

If she had done something opposite then and sent that letter, today it would be completely different. That moment could have given me a huge plus not only in my school but also in my brother's school. I could have been noticed. I could have helped someone! But I was never given that opportunity, not in that moment, nor in any other moment when I tried to reach beyond the standards set by the limitations and lack of empathy of my parents.

I was a neglected child. Although my father worked in Germany, I never had nice clothes. It's not about brand-name outfits, just about clean, new shoes, a jacket or pants. Very often I would take my clothes out of the laundry basket and go in dirty ones because my mother didn't have the time, or perhaps the inclination, to deal with it. I remember borrowing sneakers from friends and the days when I had to exercise in socks. When I didn't have a gym outfit, they would lower my behavior grade, which in turn lowered my average, which then made my mother have grievances against me. What a child feels at such moments is indescribable.

I still remember those moments when I felt lost and inferior, precisely because of those clothes. My friend's mother was an alcoholic, but she always made sure her children had clean clothes. At their home, the situation was such that they had access to clothes from a family-run store. They took clothes on credit, and later, when the financial situation was better, they paid everything off. They were resourceful; they tried and acted to ensure the children didn't feel excluded, sad, or lost. I felt that way. In reality, it was my everyday life, but the more situations in which I could compare my life to others, the harder it was for me. The doubts that appeared in my head and the feeling that maybe I just don't deserve it should never have arisen. Never in any person, especially in a child who is still shaping their vision of reality and their future self. My parents were always in debt to someone, but when I asked my mother to buy anything I needed, I had to have a really good argument. Otherwise, it didn't happen.

I also remember one situation that perfectly shows how little my mother cared about what I wanted. It was when we were going to the market for basic things. The stand in the third row, roughly in the middle, belonged to a lady selling underwear. We went there and after a while, I pointed out the colorful panties. It was probably a set with a bra in a vibrant pink or purple color.

"Mom, I would like those panties," I whispered shyly.

"What, are you going on a striptease date?" she asked immediately. "Why do you need that?"

"For nothing, I just want new panties..."

It's hard to forget that humiliating event, especially since she ultimately didn't buy them for me. I wasn't asking for anything extraordinary at the time. I just wanted new underwear. Was it so hard for her to understand that? Of course, she might not have had the money at that moment, but the basis of communication with a child is understanding their point of view and attempting a normal conversation. Couldn't she have said that she would buy them but perhaps tomorrow? That I should wait a bit because she understands that I need them. Anything other than trivializing my needs. So, I didn't get either the panties or understanding from my mother. This applied to all situations where I asked for any clothes.

I never really talked to her. An exchange of words, maybe sentences, of course, took place, but there was never a situation where I said something and a topic would start and a conversation would flow, and we could talk about our feelings, surroundings or dreams. Something like that did not exist for me, both with her and with anyone else later. It made me hide my true self deep inside, and for most of my life, on the outside, I was someone completely different.

I remember a peculiar thing that remains in me to this day as a direct legacy from my mother. We were sitting together at the table during a meal. We weren't talking to each other; she was, as usual, absent. Her unnatural posture, leaning over the table, and lively facial expressions were disturbing enough that I asked her why she was making such faces. She answered that she thinks a lot, and her expressions were simply reactions to those thoughts.

After years, I understood that she was talking to herself at those times, indeed, nodding, raising eyebrows, or pursing her lips were quite frequent behaviors of hers when she sat alone. I know this because I started doing the same in my adult life.

Even at that moment, the topic didn't continue either. She would always cut things short quickly. However, she could treat me like I was nothing and talk about my most intimate matters to strangers, without worrying whether I heard, if it would hurt me, or if I would feel simply humiliated. Once, while talking to her friend, as the friend was leaving, right by the door, she revealed that I would soon have my period, that my breasts were starting to grow, and that something was already happening. I heard all of this and couldn't believe that she was saying it. I wanted to sink into the ground. It didn't fit in my head that she would talk about such things about me to a stranger, and on top of that, not take me seriously.

This coincided with the time when I was chosen for the Miss School competition, and maybe that's what inspired her. When I told her about it, she first laughed in my face. Later, I remember somewhat blackmailing her, but out of the three required costumes, I only had one and had to withdraw from the contest. Another girl took my place, and I lost the opportunity again. I really liked dressing up, adorning myself in colorful dresses, and showing off.
She didn't understand that.

I remember that the disputes between my mother and father often, or even always, primarily impacted us. When I was five or six years old, we spent Christmas Eve in the apartment, without a Christmas tree. That year, my father decided to punish us for something. I don't even know what it was, but it was very hurtful to me at that time. Today when I ask my mother about it, she only responds briefly, so either she doesn't remember or she simply doesn't want to talk about it.

I remember a table stood between two couches. My mother and I were sitting on one couch, while my father sat alone on the other. He told us to just sit there and be quiet. It comes to mind that this was probably after my mother first stood up to him, threatening divorce, and she was severely beaten. But it could just as well have been because my mother refused to go to my father's family for the holidays. That would even make sense. If we don't go to my father parents', we won't have a Christmas tree, presents, and the celebration. Or maybe my mother didn't want to cook the twelve traditional dishes for Christmas Eve as tradition demands? I didn't understand, and it was unimaginably sad for me. It was a harsh shock. As a child, I very much looked forward to the Christmas tree and presents, and their absence was simply cruel. Then I began to think that my parents couldn't give me what was present in other homes.

I remember all the other kids were nice, polite, capable, and worthy of emulation. I was inferior in every way, which was communicated to me both implicitly and explicitly. Whatever I did, it was unnecessary, mediocre, worthless. And to add to that, my brother, with all his abnormal behaviors, was the favored one at home! And when Agatka was born, I became even more invisible. Yet, for my mother, I then became the perfect tool. A great, handy babysitter for the baby.

A relationship with a mother doesn't have to be easy, but if there's a will to understand, tenderness, and support from both sides, there's a chance to build a bond and, perhaps, longing over the years. Denying the mistakes she clearly made as a parent has completely closed off the path to understanding. This isn't about compensation or trying to turn back time. It's about understanding the past, realizing that it's worth working through it, that there were situations, moments, and even years when the much-needed support and understanding weren't there. That all of it affects life. A simple "I'm sorry" could have been a start. Without it, it's still possible to live and let go of the past, but forging a sincere, true, and healthy relationship just can't happen.

When a mother seeks happiness

Everyone has the right to happiness, and everyone has the right to seek it. However, it's important to consider others in this quest, especially those closest to us. Desperately trying to save a relationship, being in a toxic relationship, living daily in fear, and lacking joy in life—these are not good foundations for children. If a mother cannot provide her children with safety in such matters, she should do everything to at least give them a foundation on which they can build their happiness in the future. It's difficult, but conscious parenting is about giving your child as much value as possible. However, one should remember that a child does not listen, a child imitates.

I was about thirteen when my mother met her lover. Krzysiek, because that was the man's name, was in prison, and my mother would visit him there.

But let's start from the beginning.

When I was accused of stealing gold, I was also beaten very severely by my father for the first time. It was because of Wieska, who had made bold accusations. My mother had become friends with her shortly before this incident. I remember that she had two children by different men and her financial situation left much to be desired. She had a social housing apartment with two walk-through rooms, and I don't remember whether she had her own toilet or had to share it with the other tenants. She had one bed, and her children did not have too many clothes and pleasures in life. I also remember that she was always borrowing money from us. When she came to ask my mother for money, she asked that it not be mentioned to my father. And when she was pressuring my father, she would ask that my mother not be informed, and so it went. She even appealed to my father because she was cheerful and open. This friendship lasted insanely long, and I don't even remember why it ended. In any case, for a while, our daily life passed with Wieska.

At some point, my mother began to visit Krzysiek, the brother of Wieska's partner, in prison. Both brothers were behind bars for reasons unknown to me. Sztum was generally known for having a prison. In the past, it was of high security, later not so much—if you can even speak of a prison in such terms. As I think about it, that was just Wieska's way of life. She always had a man who was currently in prison, and this kind of life must have somehow fascinated my mother, who slowly began to absorb her beliefs. And eventually, indeed, she ended up visiting one of the inmates.

Interestingly, she took us with her to visit this stranger. First Agatka, then me. Of course, my father eventually found out, and one day he waited for her outside the prison gate until she came out from the visit. This was during our first move out of my father's apartment. Sztum is a small town, so such a thing was no secret to anyone. Someone might simply have seen her and told my father. Anyway, one day he waited for my mother in front of the prison gate. When she came out, they talked for a long time, and it wasn't a pleasant conversation.

When they got back together after some time, my father's family hammered my mother, constantly talking about her vile conduct. However, no one seemed to look for a motive or wanted to know my mother's version of the story. I also don't know that version; for me, all this was just another situation over which I had no control. When I went with my mother to these visits, I didn't feel any strong emotions. It was very strange to go through all those gates, but I didn't see that man in terms of a new father. That didn't really come to my mind then. I just felt strange there because there were many prisoners, and the room itself was not very cozy. I knew that wasn't my place. After all this situation, when my parents got back together, our world returned to the previously established tracks.

Continuing a toxic relationship destroys one from the inside. Promising oneself that things will get better or staying at a dead end out of helples-

sness and lack of courage to leave leads to an internal death. Not every marriage can be saved. Not every marriage should be saved. A child should not have to watch parents who not only don't love each other but also hurt each other. They will build an image of a relationship on this, which they will most likely, subconsciously, strive for.

Only End

When pain leads to destructive solutions

Happiness is a feeling that must flow from within us. It's therefore healthy to believe that we can be happy with someone by our side, as well as without someone. Unfortunately, without such role models, it is hard to achieve a state where life with someone becomes a shared journey, rather than an attempt to change our own life. Being with someone in order for them to save us will quickly bring the relationship to a place from which it will be difficult to do anything good for both parties. If we don't have anyone around us we can trust, and every day seems to us like an empty space without the possibility of grasping anything, we begin to look for a solution further afield. The lack of comfort from within pushes us toward solutions that are only seemingly simple. Why? Because we want to feel needed and loved. We want to enter a world as quickly as possible where someone will finally love us.

So there I was, more or less consciously seeking comfort in the arms of others instead of finding it within myself. Every guy I ever got close to in a way that hinted at a romantic relationship, was not exactly a great choice. Typically, the age gap was too significant, especially since I was a teenager, for anyone to consider the relationship healthy. Tomek was ten years my senior and was failing at life.

He took drugs and abused alcohol, and I fell into that lifestyle naturally and smoothly because, for the first time, I felt safe and good with someone. Even if it was through something so destructive. We often drank until dawn, reveling in the thrills of partying on amphetamine and alcohol with immense pleasure. Of course, my father disapproved of our relationship, which only made me more certain that I wanted to be with this guy. If he locked the doors, I'd escape through the window. I remember running off to spend the night with Tomek, only for my mother to be sent to fetch me the next day. I was surprised. Had he chickened out? Another surprise awaited me at home, as my father did not raise his hand to me this time. I began to think more about it and came to some conclusions.

He simply feared those stronger than himself. And Tomek was too strong an opponent. Perhaps it dawned on my father that if he hit me again, someone might avenge it. He only felt strong against those weaker than him. He was confident only when he knew no one would return those blows. He wasn't interested in confronting someone who could fight back. Was he really afraid? Probably. From that point on, he seemed to stop hitting me, but he continued to do everything to make me remember how much of 'trash' he thought I was.

When Life Loses Its Meaning

Everyday life, steeped in loneliness, pain, substance abuse, and a lack of understanding, becomes normal for a child. Day after day, they learn to live in a world that brings only suffering. Sometimes, deep inside, a flicker of hope for a better tomorrow still smolders, but often they give up. They give up the fight for themselves and their life.

I was fifteen when I started to seriously drink and use amphetamines. I didn't shy away from anything that could offer me temporary relief. Spirits were also an option, why not? The cheapest wine and anything I could buy with the few coins in my pocket. In my first year of middle school, I started smoking cigarettes, but I could usually only afford the Russian ones from the kiosk. Sometimes I would allow myself so-called 'bond' cigarettes, but not too often. I smoked non-stop, unable to quit. When I didn't have a cigarette and felt the craving, I would get nervous, sweat, and couldn't focus on anything. I remember that this was my toughest addiction. It gave me a kind of control over my life, even though I didn't realize how enslaved I was by it. The addictions stayed with me for years.

I decided it was time to end my pain. It happened right after Tomek hit me for the first time. That was the last straw. The mere thought of living on, begging each day for a breath of clean air, made my chest hurt. Every bone and muscle in my body screamed that they couldn't take the tension anymore. Disappointment with life, the lack of an escape, and the feeling of sinking deeper into it all led me to one clear thought. It's time to die. And when I thought about it, I felt peace. I didn't brag about it, and didn't tell anyone what I felt and wanted to do. The only thing I could do was take a large number of pills.

I didn't want to, and at the same time couldn't, do it any other way, because I didn't want to inflict more pain on myself. Using a knife and trying to slit my wrists was not an option; I just couldn't bring myself to do it. I couldn't imagine using a rope, as waiting for death in such a situation would be torture. I also couldn't jump out of a window because the step toward the unimaginable pain of the impact was too much for me. I was, and perhaps still am, very sensitive to pain, having experienced so much of it. Daily beatings, loss of consciousness, the lack of logical explanations for those situations, and constant uncertainty meant that if I could avoid pain, I wanted to. I didn't expect the pills to help me or that I would return to a normal life. I really wanted to die then. To disappear forever from this hostile world.

Now, in my adult life, I can only accept pain that has an explanation and serves a purpose, like the pain during childbirth. I can't accept any other, irrational, unnecessary pain that destroyed my childhood both physically and psychologically. I know that life only gives me what I can endure, but that also means that at that time, my capacity to endure that evil was already severely strained. I didn't want to feel even a single heartache. Not one more moment where I couldn't tell if it was my soul or my body that hurt.

Where did I get the pills from? Every home medicine cabinet has something a child shouldn't take, and usually, it's not very well secured. In my house, there were a lot of those pills, so I took advantage of the situation. I didn't even have to search long or choose. I found strong painkillers, my mother's liver medication, and other dangerous pills. It was almost twenty years ago, so it's hard to say exactly how many I swallowed, but I assume it was about seventy in three handfuls.

I remember that vitamin C tablets with a sweet coating were popular in Poland at one time. I loved those. Now it seems obvious to me that I liked them because of the sweetness they provided, something I couldn't get elsewhere. I could eat up to five tablets at a time, and when my mother noticed, she called me a "drug addict." Another great example of parental acumen. Didn't it occur to her that there was a reason I was doing this? As a child, I might not have needed to understand, but she should have tried to find out why. Yet there also, I could not even count on a hint of interest, only hurtful insults.

Just before that, I had another big, heavy argument with Tomek and was left alone in my room. It was one of those arguments that signaled the end of a relationship, and I couldn't imagine that. We were sober, and such a conversation without alcohol was dictated by more than just a playful high after using substances. Breaking up with Tomek meant only one thing to me. Everything that had been would come back to me like a boomerang. It's not that I would miss that person for more than a few weeks. It's that he gave me a semblance of safety and protection from my father and brother because the moment I started seeing Tomek, my brother never touched me again. Even if he was an alcoholic and perfect material for the same pathological father as mine. At that time, he gave me space and a small world where I could breathe. If he disappeared, my father would step in again. He would start beating me again, and my world and life would revert to the times when I felt so very alone. My brother would abuse me again.

During all those years before Tomek, when school and my surroundings didn't want to see my despair, bruises, bags under my eyes, and the emptiness in them, I saw no reason to trust the people around me. Tomek was the only support and constant in my life. A toxic and unhealthy relationship with him was better than my life up until then. A teenager who hadn't had the chance to grow up had no chance to work through such a situation calmly and normally. There was no chance. So if I were to break up with him, I wanted to break up with life too. There was no reason for me to continue existing.

My mother was either watching TV or asleep at the time, in any case, she had no idea what was happening. I didn't prepare anything beforehand. I just went to the kitchen, took the pills, and went back to my room. I swallowed them and drank some water. And then I waited. I didn't want to feel pain anymore. Even in that last moment on earth. Then everything happened quickly, and it turned out that the experience didn't want to miss me. I remember falling asleep quickly, then waking up to my scream.

My mother later told me that she saw me coming out of the room and heading toward the phone by the door. She felt something was wrong when I grabbed the shelf and fell. She called an ambulance, and my attempt to disappear from this world was thwarted. I struggled and resisted while the hospital staff pumped my stomach. When I woke up during the procedure, I didn't know what was happening and was very aggressive toward everyone. I didn't want to be touched, let alone have a tube put into my body. It was just a flash because I was unconscious when they took me to the hospital, and I regained consciousness only the next day. I found out that I had woken up in a psychiatric hospital, in the general ward, and the staff came to find out the reason for all this. They calmly told me what happened, what I did, and the effect of it. The confusion, the completely new situation and the surroundings made me say only that I did it because I had argued with my boyfriend. I wanted to say more, but I was so disoriented and weak that I couldn't. No one delved deeper into the topic, but luckily, I stayed in the hospital for a while.

The Gdansk Srebrzysko looked like a normal, standard hospital. It was there that I first experienced understanding and received a space where I could share with others what was happening in my life. In group therapy, I opened up and told others about the abuse from my father. During therapy, I made two friends, and this friendship stayed with me for many years.

One situation remained somewhat ambiguous in the eyes of the staff. The hospital beds were very uncomfortable, so neck, back, and shoulder pain were common. My friend and I decided to give each other a simple massage to alleviate the discomfort. In our eyes, there was nothing unusual about it. I was sitting on my friend's buttocks, who for comfort during the massage had taken off her shirt and was just in her bra. Just then, a nurse walked into the room. I can imagine how it might have looked, and the nurse's expression only confirmed it. She immediately interrupted everything and told us to get dressed and leave. Today, I just find this situation funny, but I understand what the staff might have thought.

That was a time of awakening my sexuality. This friend didn't attract me in any way, but it planted a thought in my head that it would be nice to try intimacy with a woman. During that period, my brother gave me some peace, and closeness with Tomek made me open up to these topics. It became so natural for me that I increasingly planned to be with Tomek. Those were times completely different from now when sex among fifteen-year-olds is often commonplace.

I remember that Tomek visited me, as well as my mother with my sister and my brother. I was there for about a month, during which I could walk around hospital grounds and go out to a little store at a designated place and time. I had my mother's permission to smoke cigarettes, which allowed me to go outside more often. The tranquility of that place, being far from my family and the possibility to talk about my problems, fears, and weaknesses helped me go back to a relatively normal life. I was far from being a typical kid, yet I was shown that there is such a thing as understanding. Group therapy and talking to others with similar problems were intended to help get back to normal. Yet it couldn't protect me from what was going on inside my body and my head. Not in such a short time.

No one reported what I had said about my situation, and when my father came to visit me and found out that he was one of the reasons for his child's suicide attempt, he was surprised. Genuinely, truly surprised. I was, in turn, surprised that he was so amazed. I didn't want to see him then so I refused to meet with him. He reproached me for that for many years. It was then that I realized how vastly different we are. How differently we perceive the world, emotions, showing affection, rules, boundaries, and everything that builds us or destroys us. He didn't understand that he hurt me, and I didn't understand how he could do that.

The other day, in the smoking area, I saw a girl who was in the process of gender transition. She told me that a hospital stay is one of the stages and is necessary for her to be sure that she still wants to do that. She told me about how her family supported her, that they visited her all the time. I felt more alone than ever before. I had no one who would understand me and support me, I could only dream about it. Although it is hard to tell if I even knew what support was. After that conversation, I joined a group of people who were planning to kill themselves together. I remember that we talked a lot about what we had already done and why it didn't work out. Having discussions on such things evoked in us a sense of community and peace.

Each of us knew when they would more or less leave the ward and we chose such a date that would enable all of us to meet. As a result, we planned to commit suicide four months after the moment when we first started to talk about it. Since then we would discuss in detail the exact circumstances of our plan. We agreed to meet in a forest in Gdansk. Each of us had a note with the date, the address, and the established plan. The place we had chosen was far from any roads and sidewalks as we didn't want anyone to find us. Every one of us was supposed to bring pills that we would take in a fixed order, at the right intervals and in the right quantity. The plan was detailed and we assumed each of us would end up dead.

Fortunately, after leaving the hospital I lost touch with virtually every one of them. I was involved with Tomek at that time, my father moved out of the house, and my mother tried to take care of me. She was looking for a therapist for me, she helped me to change schools and she seemed to be interested in what I felt and did. It was all overwhelming enough for the suicide plan to be forgotten.

When I left the hospital and met with Tomek, that same night we decided to get stoned again. It was an attempt to get back to the dysfunctional normalcy I felt with him. However, looking back, it was the hospital stay and the situations after leaving the ward that caused some kind of start to my healing process. It opened my eyes and many things became easier for me to understand.

They say that suicide victims are selfish, that they fail to understand they hurt their loved ones, that they cause despair and at the same time try to find peace themselves. Unfortunately, society doesn't understand that depression is a severe illness, and suicidal thoughts are powerful visions of breaking free, a sense of relief, and the end of the path filled with pain. Someone experiencing such suffering doesn't care about being reasonable. Constructive thinking about the future is hindered by recurring painful memories, which overwhelm lower and lower self-worth every day. The only sign of before mentioned self-agency at such a moment is taking away one's life. Undoubtedly, it is wrong in every way, yet a desperate person can't see any other way out. In their mind, that is the only way to find relief. They don't want to feel any more pain. Such a person doesn't see and doesn't feel that someone would cry after them, because they don't think anyone cares about them enough to suffer. They can also not feel the bond with anyone, be scared of returning to reality, and feel pain in every part of their body caused by mere thoughts. They want to disappear. Only so much and so much.

When you have to return to reality

A hospital stay is often seen as a necessary evil by many. The lack of home treatment options, poor physical or mental health, or a sudden deterioration in health are just some of the reasons that lead to a patient being placed in such a facility. Hospital buildings are associated with a sense of finality. But for many people, both adults and children, they can be a turning point.

Some might take this the wrong way, but I now see it as an adventure. I'm glad I went through all that. I met many wonderful people, and not just other patients. Psychiatrists, empathetic nurses, experienced psychologists, the environment, and the fact that someone was there to take care of me, were invaluable. It was one of the most important periods of my life, and now I can guess that everything that happened before may have led me to this place. So that I could understand that I can live differently.

When I returned to school, I saw my world and the people around me differently. Teachers, in my eyes, were simply undereducated, lacked empathy, and were bland. Stuck in the system for good.

I remember how the school system and the teachers' behavior let me down as well. Students reacted in different ways, but it was the teachers' actions that hurt me the most. And it happened more than once. When at one point I was accused of theft and it reached the teaching staff, the information spread like wildfire. The rumor started in the evening, and the next day at school, my classmates wouldn't talk to me. However, what finished it off wasn't their significant silence but the greeting from a teacher. At the classroom door, I heard something like, 'Oh, look, our little thief has arrived. Good morning, Ania.' They had no idea how traumatic that was for me. Fortunately, after my longer absence following a suicide attempt, they approached the matter somewhat differently. Maybe at least they got scared? I remember the students knew nothing about my situation, and I also got permission that if I ever felt bad, I could leave school and then talk to the school counselor the next day. And indeed, there was a moment when I took advantage of this. But when I left school, I met a classmate at whom I smiled. The next day, I wanted to talk to the psychologist, but at the entrance, I heard from a teacher that I would probably be using my permission for more truancy. I responded, confused, that I felt bad, so I left. To which she said that she saw me smiling. I tried to explain that I was greeting friends and, of course, I couldn't greet someone by throwing myself into their arms crying. The truth was, I left because I felt bad, but when I saw my friends, smiling was my natural reaction. She couldn't imagine that it was possible. A teacher with thirty years of experience in education was so limited in her thinking that she didn't know that a smile wasn't a sign of miraculous recovery.

This and many other situations showed me that school is not a place where you can receive support. Teachers are not trained to recognize and support children's emotions. There was no chance to feel understood as an individual. What kind of support could it be, when even a child who has attempted suicide receives a clear message that their smile is something bad?

Moving on from what happened was not easy for me. Forcing myself to function normally was also difficult. Unfortunately, everyday life was the same, although maybe without some issues related to beating. In the hospital, I realized that there is a different life than mine, that others also struggle with problems, and that you can come out of them and seek support. That there is such a thing as real love and support and that you can, and even should, live according to your dreams and beliefs. I learned about it, but I still couldn't assimilate it, because I was still a child, albeit a teenager, and I lived with people who brought me into this world.

Realizing that there are children in the world who only experience love after leaving their families can be painful. The closest people, even those most harmed by fate and life, should not create a world for their children in which they feel unwanted, lonely, and unhappy.

When you think about seeking reparation from parents

Going abroad for breadwinning has been and is a part of many people's lives. Sometimes personal situations, or dreams motivate us to go abroad. Why? To give ourselves a chance to earn money and improve our standard of living. Many families decide to stay abroad permanently. It's different if the trips only involve one family member, and their returns home beco-

me just visits to relatives.

Once, my mother's family asked why my father didn't take us to Germany. Why didn't he arrange for us to have an apartment and try to move us the-re? Better money, better prospects for children, more comfortable condi-tions, but that wasn't an argument for my father to make such a decision. His response was a silent, offended face, but his mother got activated like she was whipped. Full of indignation, she passionately explained how hard he worked there, how he had no time, and how much he gave us. I remember, between her one breath and the next, I retorted that he started a family to rest from it in Germany, and then a storm broke out. Father remained silent, and we listened to how he didn't need a family there be-cause he wouldn't have time for us anyway. Well, okay, but he also didn't have time for us here, so maybe it was a sense that there he might lose control over us? Or lose his asylum, his place of peace in the world? It seemed enough for him that at some point he would come to us for about four days, once every two months.

Now I know, or at least I suspect, why he didn't take us there. In Ger-many, there was no tolerance for violence against children, and it was nipped in the bud, while in Poland, most such cases were trivialized. If someone noticed that a child experienced harm, saw their torn clo-thes, fatigue, obvious malnutrition, or bruises, it usually ended with just a warning. In Germany, the punishment for a parent of such a child would be to have the child taken away. Later, when I tried as a teenager to get him to explain why he treated us that way, he dismis-sed me, saying that the past wasn't worth dredging up. It's just a pity that this only applied to memories related to how he hurt us. If the past involved alleged harm to him, he liked to talk about it, no matter how absurd it was.

Some time ago, I inquired with a Polish lawyer whether I could file legal cases against my father, mother, and brother, but at this point, they would already be considered time-barred. Maybe someday this will change since

I probably am not the only one who believes that a person who has experienced what I have should have a chance to be heard and compensated even twenty years after the last incidents. From situations that have so deeply embedded themselves in her reality and shaped her as a person. If the entire system in Poland hadn't ignored me in all the situations where it knew, today everything would look different. If I had managed to file those cases, I could see how they behave when I recount my childhood and everything they did to me. It wouldn't be my revenge, but a straightforward way to regain the necessary balance in life.

I suspect they would mainly blame me and lie about what happened to me under their roof. My father's facial expressions would probably betray him. His eyes, mouth, and face would not allow anyone to even doubt that what he says is not true, but just a clumsy attempt to clear his name. But how would he try to shift the blame for what he did to me? Saying that I was responsible for my scars from beatings? Or that I provoked his continuous beatings just by breathing?

Now I think that I could file a case only to make them answer questions. My father usually wanted to shout me down and intimidate me to stop me from talking, while my mother simply gathered her things and left. They wouldn't be able to leave from there, so maybe I would finally get an answer. And if they were judged, maybe I would finally feel cared for by this unfair system.

Escape

When parents are divorcing

No change in a child's life should occur without preparing them for the situation. Responsible parents realize that every decision they make has a specific impact on their children, regardless of their age. A conversation, an ocean of patience, and empathy are always necessary because otherwise, something will always happen that will weigh heavily on the child's future view of the world. And above all, it will profoundly shake the world in which they have to live. Parents separating is always traumatic for a child. If the child is young, they usually feel guilty about what happened and from then on live torn, without proper roots and values in life.

Sometimes there are divorces where parents soften the impact with tenderness toward the child, vast reserves of patience, and understanding of their emotions. In my case, of course, this was not present, but luckily, I was not that very young at that time. However, this does not change the fact that I was a teenager, not an adult who could properly handle my emotions.

I remember I was in junior high when I started asking, sometimes even begging my parents to get divorced. I repeatedly told them that they should divorce. I felt ashamed in front of my peers and other people because of what was happening in our home. I told my parents that it was abnormal, that they were constantly arguing, that we were always running away from this home, that they were not creating a normal family and that it was sick. And when they finally divorced years later, my father said it was my fault, that I had always wanted it.

Are you kidding me, damn it, are you trying to tell me that it's my fault that you beat my mother? That I skipped school after you hit me so hard that every part of my body hurt? That you couldn't control your own emotions?

I didn't tell him this directly, but it's pressing on my lips and maybe I should have. Would it have changed anything, though? I don't think so. His approach to life and the world clearly shows a great deal of wishful thinking and the belief that everyone and everything is out to spite him, while he's just living his life. He's poor, he just works hard, and nobody understands that.

I've heard similar affirmations of my guilt for everything when I used to vacation at my father's mother's house. There, I heard that Zbysiu was always innocent. If I wasn't the main accused, it was usually my mother, her family, neighbors, authorities, and other envious people at fault. Her son, my father, was treated as an impeccable personality, perpetually wronged by those around him. How hypocritical she was about this, only she knows, though I feel I could say quite a lot about it.

When he took out a loan for a friend, and the friend predictably exploited him and didn't pay back the loan, it wasn't his naivety to blame, but the friend's dishonesty, right? Or when my sister cut off contact with him. He doesn't know what he did to her? When I told him that he once threw her out of the house and that was enough for her, he refused to accept it. I added that I had gone through it several times, but once was enough for her and he shouldn't be surprised.

When you throw your daughter out of the house because she doesn't want to have a sincere conversation with you, knowing that she could never hope for such honesty from you, what can you expect?

There's little chance of any understanding here. Just a wall.

As for where my father lived after the divorce, it was quite unclear to me. At first, he stayed with Helena. Supposedly, she bought him a beautiful wardrobe, a fantastic table, a new bed, and provided all the comforts, because he had returned home from a terrible wife. She had to show off in the neighborhood that there was money for such expenses, and Helena's status allowed her such expenditures, especially for her son. So officially, that's where he lived. Strangely, however, he bathed at our house. Theoretically, he came to visit the children, but in practice, he just greeted us and then went to take a shower or a bath. Exactly. Now I think he didn't really need to see us at all; it was just an excuse to use our bathroom. I don't know why my mother allowed it, and I don't remember feeling resentful that my father preferred a bathroom visit over one with me. But this stemmed not entirely from his plans, but from the limitations he again encountered in his life. I remember Helena didn't want frequent baths in her house because the water bills were beyond her means. It seemed that bathing was almost forbidden.

I remember when I lived with her on weekends and spent too long in the bathroom, she would knock and ask what I was doing for so long. When I answered that I was brushing my teeth or washing my legs, she would scold me and tell me to finish. At some point, for this reason, I started going to my mother's family to bathe. They were supposed to be poorer than her according to Helena.

After the divorce, my father quickly got involved with Nina, who was his first love, and he's still with her.

Parents' separation is one thing, but their new relationships and partners are a completely different issue. Children or teenagers should not be expected to love them. Their task is primarily to look at the children with understanding, patience, and empathy, which lay the foundation for any kind of relationship. If that's not there, a hurt child is unlikely to open up, especially if they're confused about loyalty to the other parent. That's how it is in relatively healthy families. But if there were severe dysfunctions, violence, and aggression in the family, and the new parent's partner also lacks emotional intelligence? Then it's hard to talk about any positive scenario.

When a Teenager Wants to Be an Adult

Forced and rapid maturation is not a positive phenomenon. A well-cared-for child, who doesn't lack security and understands what a bond with a parent is, doesn't lose their footing even in a period of rebellion. Even if they quickly feel the urge to move out, it might be due to the desire to fulfill their dreams without necessarily cutting off contact with their family. Simply put, some children grow up faster. However, if they have to do it because of constant breaches of their safety and a lack of understanding in the family, then something is wrong. Disrupted adolescence, lack of proper role models, and violence either paralyze or force escape. Theoretically, the child thinks they are choosing a better option and maybe, temporarily, it is so. Unfortunately, how are they supposed to know what is good and what is bad? They are motivated by needs, but they can't find anything good while only emanating suffering and memories full of pain. How can they help themselves if they don't know they're still stuck in harmful patterns?

I moved out when I was seventeen. This was after my parents' divorce and during the time my mother was looking for a new partner. Initially, I thought about moving to a boarding school at the suggestion of a friend. After those court hearings, I stopped going to middle school and decided that the smartest thing would be to enroll in the Voluntary Labor Corps with a boarding section, or OHP. There were two concrete benefits for me. The first was moving out of the house, and the second was learning a trade while finishing middle school. That was the end of my relationship with Tomek, and due to my age, my parents didn't have much to say about my future anymore. So they accepted it, and my father even drove me there. He did some shopping for me, bought pajamas and a robe, and left me there. I abandoned OHP as quickly as I had decided on it. I didn't want to return home even for weekends, so I was relieved when a new guy reciprocated my interest. He was a Guinness record holder in ball juggling. He had some money, so I felt safe with him. That's when I moved near Szczecinek.

I didn't talk about it with anyone, so for a few days after moving out, nobody called me. From what I learned later, I know that my mother realized it only after a few days and then she called me. Either she ignored the fact that I was gone, or she got used to me often disappearing for a few days in a row.

This move allowed me to quickly end my relationship with Tomek, to start another four hundred kilometers away, equally damaging for everyone involved. I got involved in a romance with a guy who used me as a tool for revenge on his ex-partner. Alcohol was also one of his main problems. But again, I didn't see it. He had children, and they lost the most in all of this. Out of respect for them, I won't write who this man was. I moved in with him immediately after arriving in the city. He proposed to me in a short time, and life seemed to be getting back on track. Shared work, plans, a bed, and everyday life together. I let my guard down, only to wake up with the pain that was hiding under surface.

This guy not only used me to arouse jealousy in the partner he wanted to return to. He slept with others, practically under my nose, playing with the sincere feelings I had for him. Later, things escalated quickly. His ex wasn't interested in the jealousy because she already had someone else, so his frustration grew every day.

Fights between him and his ex in the presence of their innocent children and me were the order of the day. I didn't want to be part of it, and besides, I was no longer needed by him.

The relationship with him fell apart completely when I went to my mother's for a few days, and during that time, he didn't answer my calls. It lasted four days. I was losing my mind, and it turned out he was just drunk. At one point, his coworker called me and said he was in such a state that it was hard to even call it basic functioning.

Another failure in the emotional realm, another place to live, and seeking support in the wrong places led me into a sort of loop. I chose bad solutions because those were the only ones I knew. I created the perfect environment for such situations. The comfort zone is a feeling, a place in life where the body feels good because it knows how to behave. It recognizes the stimuli and patterns to react to. The body dislikes change, and the mind is too lazy to implement those changes swiftly and decisively. You have to engage in a tough battle with yourself and undergo a lengthy internal rehabilitation to get things straight. Deep down, I always knew this, but I still had many years ahead of repeating destructive behaviors. Because even though I internally believed it wasn't good, I didn't feel I had any other choice.

When You Return to Your Abuser

They say time heals all wounds. Maybe that's partly true. Usually, as years pass, one's perspective on one's past changes. Separation, moving, cutting off contact, and expectations about the future, maybe hope, can create an image in our heads that suits us. Unfortunately, the road to forgiveness is much longer, and the wounds left in the body and soul leave scars. There's also the force of attraction to bad situations when subconsciously we feel we need them, so our bodies can react in a familiar way. It's like an unconscious addiction of the body to pain.

I smoked like a chimney until I found out I was pregnant at nineteen. Then, for a few months, I took care of the human being growing inside me. However, once my first son was born, all my inhibitions disappeared, and I started smoking again.

Nothing was keeping me in Poland, so at some point, I decided to move to Germany. That's mainly where my father lived after the divorce. And I decided to go to him. The visit lasted only until I got back on my feet after giving birth.

Why did I do it? Because I was sure it would be better there. I had heard only positive things about life there. I was supposed to get social housing, stand on my own two feet, and just start living my own way. Unfortunately, it turned out to be just a repeat of the past, minus the beatings. Only once did my brother hit me there because it turned out he was living with my father. He hit me in the face, threatening to hit me in the stomach if I didn't shut up. Out of fear, I didn't tell my father, but slowly a feeling of tremendous exhaustion was growing inside me. I cried over my father more than once. Either he didn't like my cooking, or I wasn't learning German intensely enough, or the house wasn't cleaned the way he wanted. Nearly everything frustrated him. Again, I couldn't feel good or safe, whether he was at home or not. The heavy atmosphere was toxic, and everyday life increasingly sapped my energy to live.

Ever since I was a child, I was unsure about my father's behavior. When I returned home from school, or he came back from work, I never knew how he would act toward me. I didn't know if he would be smiling or angry, indifferent to me, or take out his current grievances on me. It was a roulette, and the worst part was that I was very dependent on this roulette. Until I saw him, there was a lot of tension inside me, which then changed directly under the influence of his behavior. It was the same later when I came to him in Germany when I was pregnant, and also after giving birth.

It was exhausting. During the week, when he returned from work at six, I somehow still functioned. I cooked, cleaned the house, and took care of little Nathaniel, who didn't sleep much during his first months of life. Around four o'clock, I would start to get stressed.

What will it be today? What mood will they be in? Will the dinner be good or bad? Will they humiliate me again and make me feel less worthy than I am?

Because of this constant tension, I was in a state of constant exhaustion. I couldn't get out of it, and the constant waiting for approval, appreciation, and at the same time constant fear of reprimands and aggression pushed me to the limits of psychological and physical endurance. Whether I was a worthwhile woman depended on whether I could cook, iron, clean, and take care of everyone around me.

Even today, I only pick up an iron on special occasions, and cooking is something I share with my partner. I never wanted to be a traditional wife, and my childhood and how my father treated me made me feel nothing but disgust for these specific tasks for a long time.

However, on weekends, I would pack all the necessary things into a bag, take the stroller, and leave for the whole day, just to avoid spending time with that man.

At that moment, when I was almost twenty years old and in my first pregnancy, going to my father seemed like the best option. Looking back, I think maybe I needed to see and experience all of that to escape from everything that kept me feeling worthless. I remember him yelling at me, demanding obedience despotically and saying things that made no sense. When my brother called me names because I was pregnant without a husband, I didn't have the energy to talk back, but today it mostly makes me laugh. Today, I'd ask him if he can't connect the dots and see the relationship between what he did to me and what he now thinks of me.

So, a few months later, I landed back in Poland, near my child's father's place. We saw each other regularly. When I returned, unfortunately, the past still followed me. My father told the whole family that I had robbed him, taken all his money from his account, cheated him, and was ungrateful. When Helena wouldn't leave me alone, constantly repeating this nonsense, I finally told her to get lost. I said that I was about to lose my patience. I added that if my father was so rich and I had only a hundred euros in my hand when returning to Poland, was that all his money? That finally shut her up. I stayed with my mother for a while, but she eventually moved out of that apartment, and I was left alone in it.

Around 2014, my mother moved to Germany. She found her place there, away from my father, and made a life for herself. I don't remember why she moved or why she chose Germany. Maybe she wanted to escape her past?

After more ups and downs, I decided to move to Gdansk, where I began my adventure with stripping. I was very determined, so I didn't give up even when I ended up in really bad places. Both the first and the next two clubs brought me traumatic experiences. Unprofessional, inexperienced club owners, dancers jealous of everything and frustrated with life, and an environment that caused me severe stress.

My determination, despite the ongoing traumas, helped me finally find a place where I could feel good. The sea of alcohol and other substances didn't bother me because I found an environment I liked and that accepted me. Stripping is still a taboo topic, but for me, it was like hitting the bullseye. That's exactly what I needed at the time. Recognition in the eyes of clients who expected a feast for their eyes. The environment gave me a lot of confidence.

Fear

When You Build Relationships on Bad Foundations

If we carry traumas and negative beliefs, we cannot build healthy relationships. The example we had as children is deeply rooted in us. We may consciously not want to engage in unhealthy relationships and assume we won't behave like our parents did. However, subconsciously, we carry many behavior patterns that we replicate in adult life. Unfortunately, we often realize this too late.

Almost until my thirtieth year, I chose partners who had a destructive effect on me. I saw them through the prism of my father. With addictions, personal problems that directly affected me, and enormous layers of various kinds of aggression. I wasn't aware that this wasn't normal, because I was soaked in such a world and only such a pattern was where I could function.

I simply never thought that a normal guy, with a job, without addictions, non-aggressive, and valuable, would want me. It was unthinkable for me because all my life I was told that I didn't deserve anything good. That I should just do, live alongside, and accept what fate gives me without complaining or grumbling, even if it was only pain, fear, and loneliness.

Tomek. My first boyfriend was twenty-five and still lived with his mother. He abused alcohol, took drugs, and completely couldn't handle life. When I was seventeen, I moved in with a man twenty years my senior. An aggressive alcoholic who could disappear for days when he went on a binge. He had three kids he didn't want to pay child support for. I was constantly surrounded by arguments with his ex-wife and her current partner. And there I was with my skewed view of the world.
Next was Pawel, the father of my older son, Nathaniel. Again, alcohol,

drugs, aggression, and theft. And in this case, a successful suicide. But he was my first love. Unfortunately, forbidden, because my whole family thought I was too good for him. Which was funny, but those were the arguments they served me. So we hid our relationship and I remember our first meetings as teenagers involved sneaking around and kissing in garages. Then we kept breaking up and getting back together until I finally got pregnant.

After all that, there was Daniel.

When You Return to a Toxic Relationship

Daniel was a former alcoholic who couldn't hold down a job. He had been in jail for vandalizing and breaking the windows of his ex's car. He was in debt everywhere possible. Eventually, he was left with nothing but a life as a homeless person in England. I met him while I was still working at a club in Sopot.

But how did I meet Daniel? My tumultuous relationship with him lasted nearly two years. Looking back, I see I ignored many clear signs that he wasn't the right man for me and that a serious relationship with him would only be problematic. I remember leaving work early with some girls and deciding to have breakfast on the beach. Walking through Monciak, we met Daniel and his friends, who joined us. After breakfast, we were supposed to go our separate ways. I remember the girls drinking with him while I went home to my Nathaniel. However, the girls gave Daniel my number, and we slowly started meeting. First, it was a beer, then more meetings. Eventually, I ended up at a party at his place and tried amphetamines for the first time. There was a lot of it, and I tried some. I remember it was a terrible feeling. That night, I also slept with him for the first time and distinctly remember feeling nothing. I was so scared that I stopped answering his calls. But over time, I relaxed, and when I finally picked up the phone, it turned out I had left some things at his place. I picked them up, and from that point, we started seeing each other more seriously. About five months later, he suggested we move in together. Nathaniel was on vacation with my mom at the time. I figured I could try it out and see what it would be like. The first four weeks were okay, but then he came home drunk for the first time. In that state, he started telling me about his past. I heard how he was abused by his stepfather as a child, how he stole from his mother, and things like that. I thought it was drunken nonsense, that it was a past he was no longer connected to. Unfortunately, I was very wrong, and all that he spoke about still deeply affected him.

One reason was that he was a very hurt child due to the abuse, but his mother gave him more reasons to be so broken mentally in his adult life. It turned out she forced him to smuggle cigarettes across the border. Cigarettes and vodka. His sister confirmed all this to me, and then I was sure everything he told me was true.

At that time, I didn't allow myself to think that I had a similar past. I know today that quitting substances like alcohol, drugs, or cigarettes pulls you back into a terrible past, into all the pain and memories you try to blur with these substances. Daniel effectively disrupted his connection with the past by immersing himself in substances at every opportunity.

My awareness was gone at that time. I drank a lot, smoked a lot, and occasionally took various drugs. My memories started coming back to me with flashbacks that appeared after I stopped drinking. However, when I talked to his sister, I had no thoughts about my past. I didn't feel that his past resembled mine. I danced in strip clubs, worked with my body, and completely pushed away thoughts of abuse, completely erasing those heavy memories in my head with drinking.

I only thought then that by telling me all this, Daniel's sister was not giving him a chance to open up to me on his terms. I continued the conversation and asked how she knew all this. She told me she caught Daniel and his stepfather in a compromising situation, but Daniel told her it was nothing, to not worry about it and not tell anyone. I then asked where their mother was at this time. I was told that the mother was afraid of their stepfather and didn't have much say in their lives. I didn't connect this story with my own, as I had completely repressed my past.

When I found out that Daniel was sexually abused by his father, I didn't realize that I also had experienced that in my childhood. I didn't think of that in this way, that I was also a victim. I was 28 when I had the first flashbacks that made me realize that. I was already in a relationship with Artur.

At that time I started to be afraid of many things; I could sense those times when I was treated as a sex toy. I was scared to lie down on the bed and bend my legs because once when I was wearing a dress and I was lying in this way watching TV, my brother was peeping at me surreptitiously. To this day I shudder out of disgust at the thought of that and many similar situations. It's incredible how long I suppressed the fact that I had been sexually abused. How much I defended myself so that it wouldn't break me. Fifteen years had passed since the moment when the abuse ended to the first flashbacks. For all that time I didn't once think about the past. It didn't happen when I worked at clubs or when I slept with any of the men I dated. My past didn't exist for me at that time, and it was a kind of shock for me when those memories started to come back.

I was with Daniel from my first club days in Sopot to Gdansk. After we broke up, I left my job in Krakow and went to England. That relationship was incredibly dysfunctional, but I only realized this after therapy and over time. Red flags were there from our first meeting, which I ignored. Unpaid electricity bills, frequent drug use, strange situations with unpaid rent, and lots of alcohol. Even when we were living in my apartment in Gdansk, it didn't dawn on me that he wasn't the right guy for me. I started paying for his therapy, and that's when I began to understand what this really was.

One day, I returned from work and gave him money for a taxi to take him to another therapy session. He took the money and ordered a taxi, which arrived relatively quickly. Something didn't feel right, so I also took a taxi and went to the therapy center. I called him:

"Hey, can you come out for a moment?" I asked when he picked up.

"But where are you?" I heard a surprise in his voice.

"Outside the center, can you come out?"

Unfortunately, I didn't get an answer because he hung up and I lost contact with him for about three days. It seemed like it could be the end, but it wasn't. I was still fooled by his pretense of commitment. Another warning sign was when he got a new job. I paid all the bills and was left with no money. I asked him to get an advance because I wanted to have some money for living expenses or to go out to the city with Nathaniel. It was supposed to be five hundred zlotych. He took the money but came home around two in the morning in a state far from normal. Tattered clothes, an empty bag, a strong smell of alcohol, and, of course, no money. I heard him as he walked down the street, yelling and waking up the neighbors with not-so-polite language. Later, he was afraid to go to the market in Gdansk, and I don't blame him. He must have been yelling and bothering various people. He wouldn't tell me anything, which annoyed me, but I slowly let it go.

My first breakup with Daniel happened in Gdansk. We had set a wedding date, but one day, after another argument, I told him to move out. I then saw him a few days later on Dluga Street in Gdansk. It hit me then that he had been homeless since. I found him tired and dirty, showing me his swollen feet full of blisters. For about two or three months, I occasionally let him come over to bathe and eat, but I looked at him without any feelings.

Right after our breakup, I felt he took advantage of me, but eventually, I understood it was my pattern. No one forced me into anything, not him either. I felt I had to pay someone to buy their attachment, affection, friendship, or eventually love. This might stem from my father trying to buy my approval after divorcing my mother. He gave me expensive gifts and large sums of money, and I felt I had to be grateful to him. He did this to show he was the better parent, not out of love for me. These situations never made me feel any more sympathy for him. I did the same, but it never brought me joy. I did it out of an internal conviction, or rather compulsion. Fortunately, now, after years of work, that has changed, and when I give someone a gift, I do it with great joy, not to make them love me.

I quickly started seeing a guy named Dominik, but soon realized I had fallen into the same pattern. The guy again earned less, got into the same trouble, and again I wanted to pay for him. I broke up with him and moved to Krakow.

Then, as I mentioned earlier, I returned to Daniel. It was a short and probably unnecessary episode. The definitive end came when one day I returned from work, lay down in bed, and he wet the bed while drunk. That was when everything that happened in the relationship with him flashed before my eyes. I saw all the situations clearly and vividly, just like the image of him running after me, dirty and tired in Gdansk. I asked myself, "God, girl, really?" I realized then that it wasn't right, and when we broke up, I was alone for several years. I also felt like a little girl again with a huge sense of guilt. I noticed my destructive beliefs and what I had done to myself. I decided to stop looking for any kind of love or relationship just to feel worthwhile. Since then, even though I decided not to look for a man, I did, but differently. I yearned for affection but didn't want just anything. I was searching for partners on Tinder, at nightclubs, and in various other places, often not even fully aware of it. Deeply ingrained in me was the belief that only by being in a relationship could I have worth, and this made it difficult for me to function otherwise.

When You Accidentally Create Something Beautiful

When you don't know who you are and lack positive feelings toward yourself, you can't choose the right person for you. You must understand that value, safety, love, and support come from within and that you must give these things to yourself. Constantly seeking them in others ultimately leads to feelings of resentment and disappointment. You expect someone else to take care of you, but in reality, your life is in your own hands.

Before entering another relationship, however, I was held back by a strong fear. During this period, I pondered who I needed and what I wanted from life. I realized that I had always been on a spiritual journey, not just recently. This realization came to me while writing this book. I was always moving forward, even without knowing it. This time without relationships was one of the most important periods, allowing me to accelerate this process significantly.

Fortunately, I eventually understood that I could live differently and emerged from this cycle of mistakes. And then I met Artur.

I chose all those partners out of fear that I didn't deserve anyone better. This was also staying in a sort of comfort zone. I knew how to behave in situations with these people because I was familiar with them. Abuse, alcohol, and substances were all that these relationships were about. There was no love, tenderness, or value in themselves. These relationships existed because being in a relationship added a bit of value to me. I couldn't find that value within myself, and seeking it externally always ended this way. The fear of something different was stronger than the need for support, understanding, or normal closeness.

My father always told me that I would end up with a bum. Funnily enough, he liked all of them. He got along with almost every one of them right away, except for Janusz, who was much older than me. Regarding Janusz, he believed that the relationship was unhealthy because of the significant age difference.

The first glance, hand-holding, kiss, and the excitement of new closeness stay in our memory for a long time, if not forever. Memories of meetings, sometimes secret ones, send shivers down our spine. Often, these first relationships don't end well, but over time it's valuable to extract the good that they brought us. Even if it was mainly another life lesson.

Pawel, as I wrote before, was my first love. When I was in elementary school, I used to write him love letters. Unfortunately, or perhaps fortunately, my mother hid them, saying he wasn't the right boy for me. I first kissed him and started dating him seriously when I was seventeen. That was when I moved out of my mother's house and into my uncle's, who lived in the same village as Pawel. My uncle's apartment was one floor above Helena's, but I didn't speak a word to her during that time.

Pawel often went on business trips, but he would come back for the weekends, and that's when we had more time for each other and liked going to nightclubs. At one point, I went with a friend to Krynica for work, for the whole summer. When we met again later, we went to a party, and that night, I ended up in bed with him and got pregnant. Things moved quickly from there. I decided not to tell him about the pregnancy and left for my father's place. I also didn't tell him who the father was. I was convinced it was the best idea. To this day, I regret it a bit because after returning to Poland, when Nathaniel was already born, I drunkenly told Pawel's mother, who commented on Nathaniel's resemblance to Pawel. That revelation caused a lot of turmoil. Some people, like Pawel's older brother, didn't believe me and suggested the truth would come out in a few years. Pawel believed me; he had no reason to doubt my words. I remember he argued with everyone who questioned them.

We cleared everything up and for a while, things were normal. We moved in together, Pawel worked, and I stayed home with Nathaniel. Unfortunately, Pawel started drinking again, and everything began to fall apart. Left with few options, I became a dancer to finally make some money.

After our breakup, Pawel still took Nathaniel on vacation and showed some interest in his life, but gradually even that faded away. Later, after we moved to Germany, their contact became very rare. Nathaniel saw his father last on his seventh birthday, and just two or three weeks later, Pawel took his own life.

A friend of mine, who had married one of Pawel's friends, called me with the news. She lived in the next village and always got information about such events much faster than I did. She asked if I knew what had happened. At first, I thought maybe Pawel got into another fight or ended up in jail again, and I said as much. But when she told me he had hung himself, I was speechless.

It was Easter, and I was in Hamburg with Nathaniel, visiting my father. After the call with my friend, I walked into the room pale as a ghost. I didn't know what to do with myself; the rushing thoughts wouldn't let me find peace. Persistent questions about Nathaniel kept popping up in my mind.

Should I tell him? What now? How will he take it? How do I break this to him?

I remember he was playing a game, and I finally called him over. I took a deep breath and said:

"What I'm about to tell you is very sad, but you need to know because I don't ever want you to think that mom is lying to you."

"What happened?"

"Your dad had an accident."

"Is it serious? Is he hurt?"

"No, Nathaniel, your dad is no longer alive."

He just looked at me and after a while said:

"Can I go back to playing now?"

Of course, I let him, and then I turned to the rest of my family who had contact with Nathaniel, asking them to stick to this version for now. I didn't want to cause him unnecessary pain. I saw no need to inform him of the details of the situation in which he had irreversibly lost his father.

Unfortunately, my mother and brother had a bright idea and, without my consent, told Nathaniel that his father had committed suicide. For them, it was obvious that the child should know this pain and not be shielded from it. After this incident, I had to have many conversations with my son to explain, among other things, why I didn't tell him everything right away. Thankfully, he took it really well. He understood as best he could, and our relationship didn't suffer. But it was indeed one of the more painful things I've experienced concerning Nathaniel. The first was his father's suicide. I knew he had to find out, but I wanted to tell him on my terms, at the right time. Wasn't the pain of losing a father enough for a little boy? I didn't understand then, and I don't understand now, why my mother acted the way she did in that situation.

It was terrible for me. I don't know, maybe she felt satisfaction that Nathaniel suffered hearing what she thought was appropriate to tell him. It was very sad. Not just what they did against my wishes, but what I felt toward them then. How can someone want to inflict additional pain on a child, especially one from their own family? Why? Why didn't they want to protect him then? And why couldn't they respect my request? I didn't feel anger toward them, just the sadness I mentioned.

Pawel came from a dysfunctional family. His father was very aggressive toward his children and wife, drank alcohol continuously, and was involved in a fatal accident during tree cutting in the forest, where his friend died. The emotions associated with that were always alive in him.

Most of the ways we behave are impacted by our parents and what they have taught us. If at some point we realize that many of our thoughts stem from the pattern ingrained in us during childhood, and to fix that we have to believe in the process of changing it even before the process begins. Unfortunately, a lot of people are afraid. Because they prefer to stay in a familiar state of mind than to get into something they have never experienced. A comfort zone is everything we live in every day. Stepping out of it is a huge step forward.

PURGATORY

THAT IS STRIPTEASE AS A WAY TO MAKE A LIVING

Introduction

The path to our goals can vary, and if we are internally lost, it can be very winding. If we do nothing to move forward, we'll become ingrained in our current place and become part of someone else's plan. It's only when we take matters into our own hands that we realize we are responsible for our lives, and it turns out it can be just as we want it to be. Usually, however, we must first go through our life lessons, which mean something different for everyone.

Working in a strip club is something you can learn. I had never danced for money before and hadn't tried to please men who paid hundreds of euros for champagne. But since I already said A, I had to say B. This kind of work has nothing to do with the colorful movies that wander around cinemas and television. Pleasing doesn't also mean fulfilling their sexual fantasies. Of course, there's always a grain of truth somewhere, but to understand it, you have to delve deeper. I know what the real competition looks like among strippers and which ones know how to fleece a client to the last penny. I know what friendships look like among them. I also know a lot about drugs and alcohol, which are nothing extraordinary in this industry. I also know what a stripper feels when she meets an old schoolmate during her shift.

Striptease

When common belief is not true

The belief that a stripper is the same as a prostitute is very hurtful. Moreover, even strip club clients think this way. Fortunately, this can be exploited. It's also worth remembering that striptease is a job. An occupation. A way to earn money. Worse, if it becomes a lifestyle and starts to permeate all other areas of life.

The remuneration system varied depending on the club I worked in. Usually, it was fifty percent from private dances and about twenty to thirty percent from drinks the client bought while with me. Tips were not accepted everywhere. In some clubs, they were returned to the bar, where they were used to buy drinks. In one club, clients bought so-called stage dollars for one euro each at the entrance, which they could then gift to the dancer. Half of the received money was given to the club.

If I knew that there were no cameras in the private room of a club, I would ask the client for a tip. Then I would receive cash from him, which I didn't have to account for anywhere, and in this way, I made quite a good extra income.

In some clubs, you could receive high penalties. This was especially painful in the Kult Club network. There, you could pay for every, even the smallest, offense. For being late, not paying by card before midnight, too little turnover, and too few drinks in a certain time. In my career, I received about three penalties. Once five hundred zlotys, once a thousand zlotys, and once five thousand zlotys for fooling around with a client.

Corona

I found the job advertisement for the Corona Club on the general access page of the Tri-City area. They were looking for bartenders, hostesses, and dancers, and I was looking for a job, so I decided to give it a try. I went to see what it would be like.

The club was located at the very end of Monciak in Sopot, where decidedly few people came. I don't know if it still exists. Back then, I remember there was a bit of a mess in terms of management. The main owner lived several hundred kilometers from Sopot. He was from Bialystok, where he had his first club. To open Corona, he had to collaborate with a certain Marcel. He was someone who probably found his worth in what he said to others. Especially to women. He also liked to throw barbs, doing it just as often as he gave effusive compliments.

Marcel rented a really beautiful space for the club. The American, world-class interior finishing was impressive. I don't know if Marcel had to renovate to achieve that effect, but one could certainly talk about a true, pleasant breeze of luxury. There was a long stage where, in addition to our dance shows, lingerie shows also took place. The stage ran through the entire club, simultaneously looking like a kind of island. At the beginning of the stage, there was a pole, followed by a wall of mirrors. At the end of the stage, there was another similar pole.

The whole place was finished in black and gold tones, and the other eye-catching point was the well-designed bar. The club had one large private room and two smaller ones, as well as a separate, well-made smoking area.

Due to purely organizational reasons and poor development ideas, it didn't function too well. The distance from the main owner's place of residence was a significant disadvantage for the club. At some point, the money that was supposed to be used for our salaries was being taken for potential penalties. That is, for penalties that we had not received but could have.

Despite the beautiful finish, excellent security, and potential, very few clients came. Initially, the club was a destination mainly for businessmen and people who didn't want to use more popular places. Here they received much more attention and intimacy, which they were unlikely to get in more well-known places, partly because of the greater risk of meeting people they didn't want to meet.

I talked to Michal, the manager, through Messenger and immediately felt that he was somewhat condescending. I didn't take it personally, as I was quite relaxed about the conversation. Only later did it hit me how he and other men were treating me. However, until about my twenty-fifth year of life, I didn't care. It was a strong feeling, not taking anything to heart, and alcohol and other substances helped with that. Looking back, I think it was a defensive mechanism for me, which stopped working after that time. In childhood, I had so many unmet needs for attention, or on the other hand, attacks on my person, that it had to develop naturally. When it disappeared and I started to care about the thoughts and words of others, I felt worse, but I couldn't do anything about it anymore.

I remember that when I later came for an interview with Michal, I started with a lie. I said that I had already been a dancer and wanted to be a bartender or hostess. I don't remember exactly, but I think I told them that I worked in a neighboring club. I also explained that there, the hostess and dancer differ mainly in that the hostess does not perform dances on stage, only in private rooms. They didn't agree with me, but I got the job. Michal said then that he knew many dancers who had moved to this job from being a hostess and didn't want to go back to the past, but I was the only one who wanted to do the opposite. I decided that okay, I'm the only one, but I want to work as a hostess or bartender.

My first shift was just observation. I was only to watch how they worked in this club, I couldn't approach the clients. I was fine with this and was pleased when at the end of the shift I got fifty zlotys for doing nothing. On the other hand, seeing that the girls were earning decently, I was a bit sorry, but I had nothing to complain about. The next night I started a normal shift and I remember that I performed about eight private dances. It wasn't big money, but they saw potential in me and I already knew I had a future in this industry.

It was only fun up to a certain point.

It ended with a situation where another girl and I were sitting at a table with two clients. Only one of them was paying, and it was clear to me that since this was the case, the earnings from this job would be divided between us two. Both of us were working on their high bill, and it was obvious to me that the compensation for this work would be shared equally between us. I had reason to think this, considering everything I had been explained and knew up to that point. Unfortunately, that's not how it happened. I was informed that the client was technically my colleague's, even though I was the one who brought him in and shared the champagne he ordered. Nevertheless, it was argued that the client wasn't mine. Several dancers who overheard this supported me, arguing that such an earning system didn't make sense. That's when things changed. Michal, the manager, started disliking me, and the main owner Andrzej also lost his liking for me.

These situations kept repeating because the club staff, who didn't know me, considered me a completely inexperienced newbie with no knowledge of the market. They didn't realize, however, that I had already made quite a few contacts. It was a time when I was transitioning from being a hostess to a dancer, and I knew a lot of girls. I kept in touch with them mainly because I wanted to learn as much as possible about this market, to see if I could handle it. Mainly because of such situations, I worked there for only about six weeks.

When I befriended Ola and Milena, Michal could approach them, even in my presence, and tell nonsense about me. They would then respond that he was behaving like a woman, not a man, gossiping about a young girl who worked for him and that without her and them, he wouldn't have a salary. They said that such behavior made them lose trust in him because they didn't know if he was saying the same things about them behind their backs.

I remember that when I used drugs with them and we all didn't come to work, he could blame everything on me. Every extreme situation or prank by a few girls was somehow my fault at some point. At first, it amused me a lot.

We all started to rebel when he began to take money from us for potential penalties we might receive. Penalties were given for anything the owners deemed appropriate. This meant that they could be assigned for being late or having a poorly conducted conversation with a client. The girls then said it was worse than in Kult, where money was taken without asking for actual penalties received. It was interesting and terrifying at the same time how easy it was for them to treat us like pawns. They took money from us without our permission, for non-existent things. That was an impulse and another reason why I eventually resigned from this job.

There was a girl from Olsztyn with a small child who worked weekends and went home during the week. And from Sunday to Monday, when she found out they were taking our money, she faced a very bad situation. She said she had a very poor weekend and needed at least enough for a ticket home. Where was she supposed to get the money from? We girls then gave her money for the ticket and some breakfast, because she was hungry after the whole night. Four of us girls also chipped in a hundred zlotys each, so she had money for food and living expenses for herself and her child for the week. When we faced such a situation, we were able to cope. I wasn't concerned about money then, and Milena had quite a bit saved up, so we weren't in dire situations. But the fact that she didn't have enough to go home was terrible. They were unmoved and had no intention of changing their behavior. Such practices were carried out with most of the girls, which was extremely unfair. There were various situations where they made a problem out of paying the girls their earnings. Sometimes they said they couldn't do it from the company account because the fee would be too high, and sometimes they convinced us that they needed the money for those damned penalties. They didn't respect our work, and in later years I met many girls who worked at Corona and were treated the same.

One of them, Dominika, had an additional business. Besides working at the club, she also organized bachelor parties. She was there when Michal was explaining the lack of payment to a girl due to too high a fee for withdrawing money from the company account.

"What are you talking about?" she burst out. "I have my own business and there's no such thing as too high a fee for withdrawing money. Pay this girl what she's owed and stop talking nonsense, don't make these girls look like fools."

He then shut up, but for some time banned her from coming to the club. After that time, she returned and everything went back to normal. Dominika was a very interesting character. I don't know what drugs she was using. At first, I thought it was crystal meth, but I must have been mistaken because the effects were somewhat different. Sometimes she behaved terribly after using them. She was quite well-known in the Tri-City area and had her reputation. Not only did she work in the club and run her own business, but she also often worked on assignments at various nightclubs. Unfortunately, either she got lost in all of this too much and no one helped her at the right time, or something else happened that I can't know because about five years ago, she died. I felt sorry for her because she had potential and could have lived a really beautiful life.

Working at Corona was tough, and we became increasingly cautious. We even developed a system where most private dances were performed for tips out of fear that we wouldn't get paid again. So, we somewhat deceived the clients, taking money from them for the first private dance in the traditional way, only to charge the subsequent dances for cash, calling them tips. We also shortened our performances; for a supposed fifteen-minute dance, we took three hundred zlotys but only danced for seven minutes. With each drink, and with each dance, our fear grew, but eventually, we realized this was not the right way to go. Milena even mentioned that it was better at the infamous Kult, where at least they were paid regular wages. At Corona, with few clients, we were constantly anxious about our earnings. It wasn't a healthy situation, especially since the club itself must have been in a difficult financial state. If we weren't earning, we didn't want to work there, and if the club wasn't making money from us, it wasn't profitable. When the money did come in, the club took it for itself and didn't pay us, so there was no motivation left for us to want to work there. At one point, strange people started coming to the club, and the girls were instructed to go to the big private room with them. It was clear that the situation was overwhelming them, as it became evident that they simply didn't know how to run the club to make it profitable.

There was also an interesting situation with champagne. The rule was that if a client didn't drink the champagne he bought, we would do it for him so that he would buy another one faster. In some situations, we could discreetly pour it out, but this wasn't possible in all private booths. One evening, I drank more than usual and, feeling trapped, also finished the leftover champagne. It exhausted me. I was drunk and could barely stand on my feet. I was so tired that I leaned on a client and fell asleep right away. I must have slept for a good while because the management noticed, woke me up, and told me to go home.

The next day, I had a day off but went to the club to collect my earnings from that shift. I was there with my friend Blanka, her child, and my Nathaniel. I had brought her to work distributing flyers and inviting customers inside. She stayed outside, and I went to talk to the boss.

Michal said he wouldn't pay me because I had received a penalty. I remember it was only two hundred and fifty zlotys, but I wasn't going to leave empty-handed. I knew that the main boss Andrzej was in the club, so I told Michal that I would talk to him. He wouldn't allow it, saying everything was already settled and there was no need. I was disoriented and in a slight shock, I insisted on getting my money. He said no. I didn't understand what was happening. I walked out and immediately told Blanka I hadn't received my money. When he heard that, he immediately came out after us. I asked him how he imagined Blanka would take the job, seeing how he treated me.

"Don't lie! You will get paid, but not today."

"But you just told me I got a penalty and there's no pay for me."

Then he ignored me and turned to Blanka. He introduced himself and started talking about the job.

"Man, are you going to pay her or not? If not, I don't want to and will not work here," she asked, slightly disgusted.

Then Michal theatrically turned to me and asked if I saw what I had just caused. It was incomprehensible to me. He hadn't paid me and blamed me for the fact that Blanka wouldn't work for him under such circumstances.

That situation was my first direct red flag. The amount in question was just two of the cheapest champagnes, so the sum was laughable, but it was my money. First, he didn't let me talk to the other boss, and second, he twisted the situation with Blanka in a way that made it seem like my fault and responsibility.

Eventually, a whole group of us girls, including myself, Milena, and Ola, moved to another club. There were eight of us in total, so this sudden change in staff, or the sudden absence of most dancers, must have been a significant blow to the owners. The club eventually closed down. I remember that I didn't take away anything from that club except for a solid lesson on who I should be working with. Who to sit with at a table, who to talk to, and who to merely exchange courtesies with. This experience made it easier for me to act later in a way that was beneficial for me. I was very careful about whom I invited to the private room and with whom I drank alcohol.

For a long time after that, I kept getting calls asking me to come back to work. They promised me that things had changed, that certain people were gone and it would be better. However, these pleas initially took the form of trying to make me feel guilty for leaving the job along with the other girls. They tried to convince me that it was my fault, that I had persuaded them, and that because of us the club had to close. Later, when that tactic didn't work, they changed their approach and started enticing me to return, promising unrealistic things. Then it turned into another form of manipulation and more pleas laced with threats and attempts to induce guilt in me. It even got to the point where they started calling the other girls and slandering me. Fortunately, their lies were so transparent that it was hard for them to achieve anything by such actions.

I never went back there. I even left behind quite a few of my belongings, which were not cheap. Dresses, work lingerie, shoes, cosmetics, and jewelry probably became the property of the next dancer, but I can only guess. However, I didn't want to expose myself to direct contact with my phone interlocutors, so I took only a few essential items and closed the door on that chapter of my life. As far as I know, the club never operated normally again. They tried to survive the first season, were ready to close the next, and still pleaded with each of us to return. Eventually, they had to close down, and now I don't know and don't care if they managed to re-enter the market. None of us wanted to return to uncertain earnings, and fortunately, all of us found well-paying positions. Who would want to return to such low wages and, above all, such deceit? The club was exclusive and had huge potential, but it fell due to a complete lack of imagination and a basic need for deceit.

Essence

The next club I worked at was located in Sopot and was really cool. It offered better money, better organization, and an atmosphere that allowed me to relax. I remember the daily fee was a hundred zlotys. The club attracted many Norwegians and employed a lot of girls.

In the middle of the large room, there was a stage surrounded by tables for the clients, while the girls usually stood by the bar. Despite the high competition, it was possible to earn well because the club was spacious. I remember having conflicts with one girl, Daria, who particularly disliked me. She would pick on me for things like choosing songs for dances. When I asked the DJ for a specific song, she would get angry, claiming she had already danced to that artist and that it was reserved for her. However, when I asked if the DJ was aware of this, as he had agreed to my request, she didn't answer. I remained calm and spoke to her rationally, without emotions. She, on the other hand, was venomous, displaying a completely immature image of a girl upset about someone stepping into her territory. Many girls witnessed our conversation. It looked as though I was calming down a little girl, furious about something trivial.

On my first night, someone broke the sole of my really good heels, the so-called "glass shoes." Whoever did it must have used a hammer or some heavy tool, as damaging them in such a way was quite difficult. These were special shoes for strippers, starting at around three hundred zlotys – a significant investment, especially for beginner exotic dancers. They had shiny decorations, and though I wore them occasionally and always kept them in the locker room, I had another pair for a change. However, I reported the incident to the manager. He acted really cool about it and reimbursed me half the value of the shoes, saying he wouldn't delve into what happened, but to avoid making me too much at a loss, he would give me part of the money. He also mentioned that he didn't know if I would want to stay with them, but he wanted to maintain a good atmosphere. He advised me not to make a big fuss about it and to come to him if something similar happened again. This made me feel safe, especially appreciating the manager's maturity, who simply showed me that it's best to act silently. I was supposed to come out smiling in my replaced shoes, and that's exactly what I did. So, the start was quite intense in this club, but everything else settled down fairly smoothly. Only Daria kept trying to bother me as much as possible, which mostly made me laugh rather than feel scared or wronged.

Daria was very beautiful, a good dancer, and she made decent money. She must have had some big complex to treat me that way. Fortunately, despite the emotions boiling inside me, I remained very calm, which helped me a lot in many potentially critical situations. Because I didn't react rashly or impulsively, I could often ignore her aggressive snipes.

I made good money there and gained a lot of useful experience. It was a great club for learning. If I didn't want to approach a client, I didn't, and if I did, I did. The best earnings were on weekends; during the week, there were significantly fewer clients. I had a strategy of approaching the same client multiple times, as it usually meant a higher chance of earning more. I wasn't interested in unproductive sitting at the bar. I worked there for several months, but looking back, I can say that despite many advantages, the Esencja Club also had a few drawbacks. One of them, in my opinion, was the excessive number of dancers. However, from the management's perspective, this was a plus. When potential clients see a large number of girls, they stay. When they see few, they simply leave.

The situation with the shoes reminded me that I had never had such a nice, valuable relationship with another woman. In school, in middle school, all the girlfriends or acquaintances had relationships based on some benefits. So why did I expect something different in a strip club? I remember when I got home and took the shoe by the heel, my surprise and disappointment were big. Someone wanted to get rid of me from the club, and it was hard for me to think of anyone other than Daria.

There was also an incident with a girl, Marzena, with whom I thought I got along well. When an interesting client appeared, we would call each other to the room to boost our earnings. I felt like she was my friend, just like that. We never went out together or spent time outside of work, but our contact was very okay. One day, I went to a cool sex shop to buy shoes and met her there. She was with her friends, one of whom was buying some stuff for a bachelorette party. When I entered and was happy to say hello, her sudden behavior quickly cooled my enthusiasm. She immediately made up an excuse to go outside to smoke and hurriedly informed her friends. In a second, I understood that she didn't want me to greet her there. She didn't want to admit she knew me. She panicked, but her friends didn't understand what was going on, especially not connecting her behavior with me. I was surprised, but I came for the shoes and just bought them. I was still quite naive at the time and believed that the girls I worked with were sincere and not deceiving me with their behavior at work. I went home by streetcar, as the traffic jams in a taxi were not pleasant. She had the night off, but I talked about the situation with another girl. She told me that many of them behaved like that because they didn't admit to their close ones and acquaintances what they did. This made no sense to me.

What do you tell them? You're not home five or six nights a week, you sleep until the afternoon, live differently than with a standard job, and additionally, you constantly lie about your life. You have a messed-up lifestyle and still keep making things up.

I had friends outside the industry, one a nail technician, another a hairdresser. What was I supposed to tell them when I opened the door, sleepy again? That I party every day? How much energy would I have to spend living in constant lies, constantly creating a facade? That wasn't for me. Definitely not.

The next day, Marzena came to work and, without even saying hello, began loudly mocking me for moving around the city by streetcar. She laughed aloud, but alone, as no one else saw anything so odd or funny in it. Maybe she wanted to turn the situation to her advantage, maybe she was embarrassed, or maybe she couldn't find herself in it. In any case, her attempt to ridicule me in front of the other girls didn't quite work out.

I responded directly, recalling situations from my middle school days, now quite angry:

"Hey, I take a streetcar, but who doesn't during peak traffic? Tell me, is your refusal to greet me yesterday because you're ashamed of what you do? Would your acquaintances not accept you if they knew the truth?"

Then she almost jumped at me with her hands, unable to handle it. I realized then that our relationships were very superficial and dancers befriended each other only to earn more.

Venus

The law of attraction and manifestation was with me every day. When I left home for a shift, thinking that I would earn a thousand zlotys, I always did. Whenever I needed it, I earned or received it in some other way. And it wasn't just close to the amount I manifested. When I said I would earn two seven hundred, I earned two seven hundred. When I said I would drink four champagnes, I drank four champagnes. I don't remember a day when it was different. I just remembered to be precise in my wishes, as I preferred the most expensive champagnes, not the cheapest.

One of the owners of the Kult Club chain had the Venus Club, which was all about effectively making money. There, there was no choice, and the work rules were very strict. The shift manager pointed out which client we had to approach. Moreover, we had to sit with them until the end of their party if they bought anything. As a result, there were frustrating situations where, for example, one girl had to accompany a man who had only bought a fifty-zloty drink. Another girl sat until noon while the client bought her two cheapest drinks per hour, so she earned about thirty zlotys per hour. That was a downside, but I started to earn well there. And I felt what real jealousy was. The girls there were so beautiful and aggressive in behavior that every newbie had a hard time with them. I didn't let them walk all over me from the start, and because I was constantly arguing with them, I had a tough time, but many new dancers simply couldn't stand the atmosphere. It could be freely called mobbing, which was allowed by the shift manager Daria. She looked like a small, happy overweight woman. Long, gel-crushed hair was supposed to imitate curls, but with poor results. Very insecure, malicious, and nasty. And also drunk every night.

Every night we had a meeting where current issues were discussed. All the girls tripped each other up, gossiped, and accused others of unpleasant behavior. If any of them did something wrong, she was immediately branded and punished. And Daria hunted for such girls. Often barely balancing on her chair, she still growled and attacked the girls, always looking for culprits. After about two weeks of observing what she did to others and how she drank, I completely lost respect for her. She couldn't handle herself, yet she tried to straighten us out. She picked on everything. I left the table too quickly, didn't try hard enough, did something too slow, too fast. Not as she deemed right.

For the first month, I was bothered by everything and had a combative attitude toward both Daria and the other girls, but I soon got over it. I stopped getting emotionally involved in what they were doing, while internally laughing at those unnecessary altercations.

When I got up on the wrong side of the bed and was inexplicably angry, I usually ended up arguing with a bartender or another dancer on my next shift. This was especially common in the club Venus. This club was so saturated with negative energy, jealousy, and anger that it just had to be. The club was necessary for me to learn how to navigate this world, but also to understand my worth and learn to live with others' opinions without letting them affect me. In subsequent clubs, rude remarks and provocations no longer bothered me, but in Venus, I went through a tough, substantial school in this respect. Today, I probably wouldn't even hear those things, but back then, they were a quick trigger for another aggressive exchange.

Once, I was sitting with a client who spent over seventy thousand zlotys on me that night, of which twenty-five percent was for me. In this club, waitresses often helped us, but that time, one of them seemed panicked that I would take everything for myself because she approached the private room table several times and suggested bringing in another girl. The waitress spoke to me in English, and the client responded in the same language. There was a suggestion to bring in my colleague, but he initially refused and then several times said that if someone else came into the room, he would leave and stop paying. And that's what eventually happened. As a result, I earned all the money related to that client. At the meeting, the same waitress tried to convince others that I didn't want to let anyone else earn. I remember that I told them to check the cameras, and then she shut up. I told them not to manipulate the situation because it was clear and didn't need any tampering. At one point, they accused me of not letting Ola, who had helped me with another client, earn money. A few days earlier, she called me to the room, and we earned a lot together. Not wanting to cause Ola the ordinary displeasure of thinking I could have but didn't let her earn, I simply repeated that it could be checked on the cameras. That was the last situation where I argued with them. In subsequent instances, when they tried to slander me, I just told Daria to think and do whatever she wanted. I suggested she fire me if she thought my behavior was inappropriate. I said I was tired, I had made my money, and I had no energy for any quarrels. If they wanted to deprive me of any money, they had to prove I earned it dishonestly. I also told them they had no chance of dragging me into such primitive arguments. This pissed them off so much that at one point none of them talked to me anymore, which suited me just fine.

The waitresses didn't like me. I didn't show that it affected me, but inside I felt immense discomfort. One day, they decided to make this more painfully clear than they did every day. They started sabotaging every chance when I managed to persuade a client to buy champagne. For about a week, they approached me every time they saw that I might earn something. One night, I was sitting at a table with three different clients, and a waitress, toward whom I felt a particular antipathy, approached. She ruined my chance to earn three times in a row. This meant that she came to my table with total disregard and did everything to ensure the client didn't spend money on me. A lot depended on the waitress; the nicer she was, the easier it was to convince the client to buy another drink, champagne, or dance. At that point, I had enough.

It was a tradition in this and a few other clubs to have a meeting after each shift, where we could tell others and the shift manager about events we thought were significant. I was so angry that I decided to vent on that one girl. In a very raised voice, I said I didn't know how she dealt with other girls, but working with me was a disaster. I knew that when she approached my table, my sales would die, her presence was a hindrance, she didn't know what she was doing and it meant no chance of making a sale. I gave an example of how when I showed a client where his wallet was, she grabbed my hands and argued with me to take my hand away and not show him anything. Such and many other behaviors caused clients to lose the desire to make any purchase. As I spoke, my voice got louder and my fury grew. When I finished, there was a deadly silence, the only response to my complaint. The girls must have been in shock. Maybe for the first time, someone had so explicitly and openly criticized their terrible behavior. Anyway, from that moment on, things got even worse for me there. There were penalties from the manager, probably to show me my place. When waitresses approached me, I started handling the transactions myself. I took the terminal and managed every transaction myself because I didn't want the waitresses to create a toxic atmosphere around payments. However, this wasn't sustainable in the long run, and the pressure and stress related to that place were getting to me. I concluded that I couldn't work with a group of girls who couldn't handle their emotions. I left and headed to the next club.

Obsession

I was drawn to this club by a girl who had worked with me at the Corona Club, but I only stayed there for a month because it was a repeat of my previous experiences. I told Milena that I left Sopot precisely because of the constantly tense, toxic atmosphere, and I didn't want to get into that again.

The manager in this club was around twenty-three years old and didn't have much control. Kate, as she was named, couldn't direct us to clients with whom we felt most comfortable. One girl felt better with older men, another preferred guys in tracksuits, while a third worked best at bachelor parties. Kate seemed not to understand this and sent us wherever she deemed appropriate. Additionally, she competed with us and could say during end-of-shift meetings that even while a dancer was sitting with a client at a table, he was still glancing at her. One day, one of the dancers became a victim of another internal conflict with the manager. Kate accused her of giving her address to a client. This client had fallen in love with Kate and wanted to find her outside of work hours. He even hired a detective to locate her. This detective found Kate's email and address, and she reportedly received some threatening emails. Eventually, she reported this to the police and found the man after some time. Despite having evidence in hand, she focused on spreading a disgusting accusation that one of the dancers was sharing her personal details with clients. I also didn't have a strong rapport with her. At the very beginning, I asked her to direct me only to older clients, as I did best with them. However, she either spitefully or thoughtlessly directed me to younger ones. I mostly felt sorry for her, because, at such a young age, she seemed out of place in a strip club.

After a month, I told her that I didn't want to take anything from my potential, but I couldn't force her to do anything, so I would leave after the next weekend. I also said that our collaboration made no sense, because if I tell her which clients I earn the most with and she ignores it, what's the point?

I was glad to quickly find another club, as I didn't want to work in a place where I felt a huge emotional distance. I mostly saw girls there who needed psychotherapy, not sitting in a club and constantly earning money. Taking out frustrations on others, a complete lack of emotional control, and unhealthy situations before, during, and after work couldn't bring anything good.

During one shift, a client bought champagne so that I would accompany him to a room. The champagne equated to twenty minutes, and that's how long I planned to stay unless he bought something else. After about twenty minutes, a waitress came in, and after a somewhat unpleasant conversation, I suggested we try to get more out of him. She agreed, but when the client wanted to use his card, he had trouble with the PIN. The waitress suggested I help him. I was a bit drunk and didn't catch the trick, so I took the terminal and entered the PIN for him. This turned into a big issue because we weren't supposed to help clients with payments by entering PINs, or touching wallets, or cards. However, the situation was tricky because waitresses were supposed to monitor the dancers. If a dancer was very drunk, it was the waitress who was responsible for what happened. So, it seemed like the waitress was in cahoots with the manager. They wanted to create a situation where I had to be fired, just so I wouldn't leave on my terms. Not only did she come before the twenty minutes were up after buying the champagne, but she also told me to help the client with his PIN. Looking back, it seems obvious. I remember leaving the room because the payment ultimately didn't go through. Interestingly, right after I left, the manager was waiting for me and happily announced that I was fired for entering the client's PIN. Still drunk, I just said thank you, that I could leave and calmly go to another club, that I could finally work normally and thanked her very much. She looked at me surprised, and I went to change, wished the girls all the best, and just left for home.

Kult

Kult starts with Esencja in Sopot. Esencja in Sopot was founded by a guy nicknamed Wrona. He opened it after falling out with Karol Nowakowski. All his clubs operated, or still operate, on similar principles.

There was something called "Pretty Beer" in these clubs. Vodka was added to the beer to knock out the client faster. This was a common practice as opposed to the rumor that said drugs were added to clients' drinks. That's more of a fairy tale because it simply wasn't profitable. Any client who had doubts would get blood tests, and none of them ever came back positive. Drugs were prohibited in these clubs, and unannounced audits and random drug tests among employees allowed for proper control in this area. Of course, that's not to say there were absolutely no drugs. In clubs where relationships between dancers were better, we tried to cover for each other. Often, when I wasn't using drugs, I would volunteer for the test so that another girl who liked to smoke weed or had just bought good coke could feel safe.

The boss of Kult was quite an interesting person. I even chatted with him on Tinder, but we never met because we had a problem choosing a place from the start. I suggested a restaurant where I wanted to try duck. He said that wouldn't work for him because he was fasting. I replied that he could just order juice, and I would eat the duck. He also didn't like that because he didn't want to watch others eat while he was only drinking. During our correspondence, he didn't even know that I was one of his dancers. On the day we were supposed to meet, he kept calling me. Initially, I didn't want to talk to him and just didn't answer, but eventually, I replied to his text asking if the meeting was still on. I texted back, apologizing, but I couldn't meet with financial fraudsters, as I was his dancer and he hadn't paid me all my due money. He then asked if really nothing was going to happen that day. His message made me not want to continue texting, as he either didn't read my texts or didn't understand them.

There was also another situation involving a different girl. While I knew he was my boss during my contact with him, she didn't. When she saw him and he stayed overnight at her place, there were many situations where she felt very confused. He was greedy and didn't make himself clear to her. One night, when he stayed at her place and she left her clothes in the bathroom with some money in them, the money was gone in the morning. He simply took it when leaving for work or wherever he was going. One day she came to work and told us about him. At one point, she showed his picture and we made her realize that he was our boss. She was very surprised.

He is an interesting man in many ways. Let's consider his past. He came out of prison, where he had been incarcerated for minor frauds related to his previous family business. A man who now had significant influence had previously spent several years behind bars for theft or other unlawful conduct. After his release, he immediately opened several clubs in many Polish cities and started cheating the dancers.

Upon starting to work with Kult, the girls had to open an account in an unknown bank. The trick was that even after receiving their salary, they could expect it to be withdrawn at any time. It got to the point where if they knew the salary would be in the account at exactly 2 p.m. on Monday, they would stand in line at the ATM to quickly withdraw it. Unfortunately, not everyone managed to do so. In Kult, there were hefty financial penalties for poorly painted nails, inappropriate makeup, and untidy hair. For absence from work, for being late, for leaving a client too soon, for inappropriate behavior in the private room, for not using a card in transactions. Generally, it was a roulette, and everything depended on what the management liked or didn't like on any given day.

My biggest penalty was five thousand zlotys in Krakow. It was another night when I had to stay longer in the club because the promotion wasn't bringing anyone to us. It was such that if we made a large turnover one night, the next night had to be similar. This was impossible, and we often feared that if, for example, we earned too much on a Saturday, the next day would start with penalties from the morning. On Saturday, we could earn a lot, but on Sunday, the traffic was minimal. However, this didn't matter to the central office.

That day I told the manager that I was really tired. It was the third night in a row where we had to sit three hours longer, during which we couldn't sleep. We had to sit quietly and wait. I then went from Karol to another club, just for a few nights. Unfortunately, Karol and Wrona didn't get along well because their previous cooperation ended in a rather difficult atmosphere. Wrona had allegedly stolen from Karol, causing a minor crisis in their business and the creation of new, but separate, clubs. No one will get to the truth, but it's said that Wrona opened his clubs with stolen money.

I worked for Wrona, but I wasn't earning much, so I went back to Karol. I was honest with them about the situation, and they agreed to my return. Despite the official approval, I felt significant pressure and knew that sooner or later I would receive a large penalty. And that's exactly what happened. The reason was evidently far-fetched. I received a penalty for aggressive behavior toward a client in the private room. The aggression was supposedly pushing him onto the sofa just before performing a dance. I remember that night well, and it had nothing to do with aggression. Before entering the room with the client, my colleague and I played his wife who yelled at him to spend money, as that was what excited him. Then, when I entered the room with him, I typically placed my hand on his chest and pushed him onto the sofa to sit down. Then I sat on him and started my dance. This was interpreted and commented on as aggression.

At that point, I knew I would leave, but good relations with the girls and the state of the job market at the time held me back. I had the choice to stay and pay the fine, or go elsewhere where it could be just as bad, but still pay the fine they would withdraw from my account. I chose the lesser of two evils, a place I at least knew. Staying gave me a false sense of security, but it was some sort of security nonetheless. It was very hard for me, and I harbored a huge grudge against them for the fine. When I found out about my penalty, I was sitting with Monika, my manager, eating burgers near the club. She received a text that a fine had been imposed on one of the dancers for aggressive behavior in the room about two weeks earlier. She told me about it, loudly wondering who it could have been. It was a real puzzle for me because none of us behaved that way. It never crossed my mind that it could be about me. However, it was a thank you for my temporary escape to Wrona, not a penalty for the mentioned situation. I remember feeling dizzy because such a sum was astronomical for me at the time.

When I worked at Kult, I also attended so-called conferences where girls from different clubs shared their experiences. There was also the head of the central office, Sylwia, in front of whom we couldn't just be honest. For example, I was supposed to attend these conferences only to talk about how great it was to work there. I had to praise the earnings, atmosphere, staff, everything. Current grievances were resolved in the privacy of the club or outside it, like at lunch.

Working there at the time, despite the poor conditions of cooperation, was one of the better experiences for me, thanks to Monika. As a manager, she was the best possible option. She had intuition, was empathetic, and honest. Under her direction, the girls felt cared for, safe, and fairly treated. The central office tried to ruin this at every turn, but it was livable.

Interesting Client

There was a group from Norway when I was working in Gdansk. They came to celebrate a bachelor party. There were five of them, dressed in yellow suits and rather expensive shoes, so we started with a shot in each of their beers. At some point, we girls divided up, and each of us took one to a private room. In my room, there was a fake flower, and when I went out to get the payment terminal, it was used in an unusual way. When I returned, I found the client urinating into it, so I left, somewhat disoriented, and waited for him to finish. When I came back, I gave him the terminal to pay for the champagne. It was about five thousand zlotys. He paid, and then, sitting on the sofa, leaned to one side and defecated in his pants. I asked the central office what I should do in such a situation because Norwegians often liked to go to the police. They immediately said that despite this, security should throw him out because no one should treat a private room like a toilet.

 About twenty minutes after sleeping outside the club, the infamous client called his friends, and they all came out for him. Incredibly, despite messing up his pants, he wanted to return to the club. To do this, he blended in with his friends and the currently entering clients and simply re-entered Kult. When the security guards saw him, he begged them to let him in. They told him to wash and change, but he only replied that it didn't bother him. I remember, when I left my shift around 6:30 am, returning home, I ran into him in the old town. It was about five hours after the whole situation. This man was determined to have a good time that night. He didn't understand why no club wanted to let him in anymore and ended up on the old town streets.

Aggressive Client

The only situation when a client was aggressive happened in Gdansk. It was the only time I felt truly threatened throughout those years. The club was empty. Apart from the staff, there were no clients. Suddenly, two Norwegians entered. One was the bodyguard of the other, and it was clear that they were dealing with big money. The bodyguard had ears typical of boxers and was massive. He had piercing blue eyes and radiated a lot of aggression. Eventually, the other guy calmed him down, paid for him, and we could proceed. He asked us when there would be sex, and as usual, we didn't answer directly, just took him to a private room. We started dancing, and after about two or three minutes, he began touching us, pulling, grabbing different parts of our bodies. We warned him that if he continued like this, he would have to leave.

"My friend didn't pay all this money for some stupid dancing," he said, standing up, grabbing me by the neck, lifting me, throwing me against the wall, and holding me there.

He looked into my eyes for a moment and time stopped. Then he suddenly let me go.

"You can keep dancing. I'm sorry I did that," he said.

I responded that I understood he might have been upset, but what he did was not allowed. The fee was paid for a dance, and his friend, who was in another room, had no problem with that. I added that they paid for twenty minutes and champagne, so he could sit in the room for that time, but my colleague and I were leaving. As I was speaking, I stood by the door, ready to leave. Security had already appeared next to me. He jumped up and stood a step from me. Jessica hid behind me, protecting her recently operated nose, and I didn't know what to do. I was in shock because, in all my time dancing in clubs, I had never encountered such a person. Since my childhood, I had been unaccustomed to aggression, and this was a mix of fear and shock. He was visibly seething with anger, and at that moment, he didn't yet see that security was standing next to us.

"I don't care how much security you have here and how many girls are standing behind you, but if you don't do what I tell you, I will simply beat you up," he said.

He said a lot more, but I don't remember exactly. Fortunately, security was indeed behind me, and the situation didn't end tragically for me. What remained was a vivid memory.

Persistent Clients

There weren't many aggressive clients, but there were often persistent ones who wanted to put their hands everywhere. We always had to keep an eye on their hands. Fortunately, I had a great relationship with Monika, the manager, so she only sent me to clients who were a good fit for me. She also didn't let anyone walk all over her. When a so-called creep came to the club and the central office ordered to send a dancer to him, Monika refused. She said she respected the girls too much to make them sit with someone like that, and if the promotion was bringing such clients to the club, she suggested the central office should try spending time with them themselves.

Once, the boss ordered a promotion where clients could drink all night for just under forty zlotys. As a result of this campaign, the club attracted a clientele from dormitories and people who did not have much money. Sometimes the club was filled with people who were not very valuable to us. The worst was when a promising group of Norwegians couldn't enter due to lack of space. It was a really bad idea, but the central office typically didn't admit the mistake and continued the campaign. We had to fight against it for a long time. During the promotion, the people on shift received money for every entrance, but they were under the threat of penalties. These penalties evolved and were a really serious matter because you could get them for generally too few entries, or if the right number of people didn't show up in the club by midnight. Later, there was also a penalty given to the manager for not having enough card transactions by midnight, or one divided among the whole group for not achieving the set number of dances. It could be even five thousand zlotys for, say, ten dancers. It was a vicious cycle that generated completely nonsensical situations.

The dancers were supposed to get penalized for not earning anything, but they didn't earn anything because the promotion didn't bring in the right number of people.

At one point, we felt that either they were having some major financial problems or they wanted to earn as quickly as possible on us, to not pay us the commission due and quickly close the business. And that turned out to be true. When I went to Krakow, I started receiving messages from the girls confirming this. I also learned that the central office located in Krakow had well-placed bugs in all the clubs and often based on what they heard, they gave penalties to the girls. The girls also told me much more about the illegal practices of the management against the dancers. Then I learned about visits from bailiffs and situations where the staff hid and pretended that no one was there so that unwanted guests couldn't figure out what was happening.

Gangster's Club

In Kult, transfers to other clubs were mandatory. This meant that when bigger events were happening in another city, dancers were sent to support them. I wasn't often sent elsewhere. Monika, for instance, kept me with her because I earned well and had a child, so traveling was problematic for me.

One day, I decided to give it a try and volunteered for the next transfer opportunity. This transfer was to the notoriously bad Poznan. I wasn't too worried about it, as I didn't believe the rumored actions that supposedly took place there. I had heard that even the security guards were afraid to come in for shifts. However, when I went there, I was shocked. The club's queen was a vulgar, rude woman to the clients. She was favored for completely incomprehensible reasons.

One night, after I had already earned about two thousand and was relaxed, I started chatting with other dancers. It turned out there was a girl I had previously worked with. Around five in the morning, as we were getting ready to go to the locker room, the manager came in and ordered us back to the floor until specific clients left. We didn't understand why we had to do this. It turned out that some gangster had bought the cheapest champagne and demanded all the girls return to the floor. Otherwise, he threatened to break all the chairs or do something else equally damaging to express his dissatisfaction. So, we had to stay until about 7:30 AM, unable to talk, laugh, or do anything that might upset him. The manager warned us that he was a very dangerous man and that she was afraid of him. I remember being just annoyed because it wasn't my club and I just wanted to go to sleep. I didn't want to cause trouble or get penalized for leaving early. I also learned that the gangster was connected to the vulgar dancer, which was probably why she could do whatever she wanted.

When I finally left the club, I texted Monika that I wanted to return because I was scared to work in that club. She replied that I could decide for myself, but if I quit, we would both get penalized. I knew what I was getting into, as everyone had explained it to me. I just didn't want to listen. In the end, I stayed in that club not to cause trouble for Monika, but it was very hard, especially sitting for several more hours without a chance to earn. I also realized then how good I had it in my club. It was the worst weekend of my entire career, or rather two days of work. Fortunately, on the third day, we ended up in a different place where both the atmosphere and the girls were really okay.

My contact with Black, the vulgar girl, was minimal, but I wasn't afraid of her. Generally, she danced very well, but offstage, she behaved more like a man. Her loudness and behavior toward clients irritated me, so I didn't intend to have much contact with her. I remember when I took a client to a private room, a waitress came after a short time to ask if we should call Black. I told her that if I needed someone, I would call a girl from the club I came from. I also explained that my client was calm and didn't need such a loud dancer. In the locker room, Black looked at me from the corner of her eye but didn't say a word, and I pretended not to see it.

Haunted Club

Another transfer I made out of curiosity took me to Lodz. This time it was during the winter period. The club was haunted. Several unpleasant stories were associated with the place where it was built. It was said that children who were taken to the extermination camp used to stay there, and the space itself was imbued with the sadness and despair of those captured. Previously, there was also a pharmacy in the same location.

A chilling curiosity was related to the visions of clients. Many men asked for a girl dressed in a long, white dress, with blonde hair. None of the staff had seen such a girl. Only the clients maintained that she was one of the dancers, according to them. This request was repeated by several people several times a week.

    The club had a large hall and a long corridor, with entrances to cloakrooms, toilets, and several other rooms branching off. There, sometimes, a running girl was seen. Glasses fell off the bar by themselves, and yet I went there. Or rather because of that. The girls in Lodz earned very little, and I wanted to see what was happening there. I wanted to feel it.

    That club indeed had dark, heavy energy. It felt like descending into a basement. During that time, I didn't see anything, but during my shift, when I was sitting at the bar, the blonde girl in the white dress was called again.

    Similar things happened in one of the clubs in Gdansk, about half a year after my transfer to Lodz. In the spring. Earlier, the same location housed an executioner's headquarters. One night, a man from Sweden came, who told us he was a medium and saw many women and children there. He said he wanted to enter the cellar through a specific room, which he pointed out. He also said that he saw a dead child near my manager, which she confirmed by admitting to a miscarriage. From that moment, I was afraid to enter that room, so I simply avoided it. It was small, with a mirror, a table with a button to call a waitress, and a small sofa. The mirror was on the side of the entrance, which instead of a door had a red curtain. To the right were the doors to the cellar, hidden behind a large flower.

Two or three weeks after meeting the Swede, I had to enter that room with a client who promised good earnings. I entered, placed champagne on the table, and sat on the client's lap. After about fifteen minutes of dancing, I leaned toward the table where the button to call a waitress was. That night, Sandra, a petite waitress with long, black hair, was supposed to come to me. I pressed the button and waited. After a few minutes, I saw a figure in the mirror similar in stature to Sandra. I didn't stop dancing, waiting for her to start the procedure. After a while, I saw that there was no one in the mirror, so I asked the client for a moment and left the room.

I found Sandra in another room, settling another client's bill. She told me she would be with me in a moment. When I replied, surprised, that she had just been with me, she denied it. So I don't know what I saw then, but it wasn't Sandra. From that moment on, I was much more cautious, and it turned out that this happened quite often to different girls.

I often worked with Sandra because she was determined, and when she came to replace me in the room, I knew that the client would pay. We had similar strategies with clients, and our cooperation was simply effective. One day, as sometimes happened, a client's card stopped working, so we had to go to the ATM for cash. I got dressed, and Sandra and I went there together. The client withdrew the money, and we returned to the room, where Sandra left the terminal on the table. No one entered the room during that time, but we noticed something strange in the terminal. Namely, the amount of six hundred sixty-six zloty was entered.

After reviewing the surveillance camera footage, the central office confirmed that no one had entered the room during that time, let alone touched the terminal. This was just one of many situations that no one could explain.

Friendship in Gdansk

The law of attraction exists, and like the law of gravity, it's invisible but very powerful. It works even when we're unaware of it. It means we always draw energy similar to our own toward us, and it's inevitable. It's a natural, absolute process that can be used positively, but one must know how to do it. I see now that throughout my life, I attracted people who, despite having a similar life and making similar mistakes to mine, had a tendency to constantly criticize me in every aspect of life. Unfortunately, I couldn't get out of those relationships because I didn't feel they were bad for me. They drained my energy, disturbed my sense of self-worth, and often made me see myself through others' eyes. I couldn't free myself because I was the one attracting them. You have in life what you are.

One day, a beautician came to my house to do my lashes, nails, and other services that I didn't feel like going to a salon for. After night shifts, my body often refused to cooperate, and leaving the house was simply too much effort. She had visited me before, and as it happens with such services, we talked a lot. About various things.

I remember one day she asked why I woke up so late. I told her I was a dancer and worked at night. From that moment, she tried to moralize me, and after each visit, I felt completely drained of energy. However, I didn't end this acquaintance because I was used to people around me doing exactly such things, and it seemed natural. In hindsight, however, I see that this acquaintance primarily served her. With each visit, she performed several treatments, so I paid her quite a lot. After some time, she pushed her mother onto me for house cleaning, who soon came to me asking for a month's payment in advance because she wanted to buy a new washing machine. That was okay for me, but the worst part was allowing her to tell me how I should dress, as she wanted. That I shouldn't wear dresses because she didn't like them, that some of my clothes were completely inappropriate, and so on. When we went out together, because this acquaintance went far beyond cosmetic services, it brought me no joy. I kept in touch with her because I thought I should.

The funniest thing is that after some time, it turned out that she didn't just work as a beautician, but one of her sources of income was being a prostitute. That really saddened me. I thought she was good, that she didn't lie and wanted the best for me. I remember confronting her quite quickly but without aggression about this information. I asked why she had repaid my trust with such a thing. I wanted to know why she hadn't told me anything and why she criticized me so harshly for being a dancer. During the conversation, she became so heated that our contact broke off for about six months. During that time, her mother still cleaned for me, so I knew she was taking various beauty courses and developing in that direction. At some point, a man appeared in her life who helped her open a salon. She had hairdressers under her and called me to ask if I wanted to be a model for hair extensions. I agreed and was happy that she called. When I appeared in her salon, I waited until we were alone and asked her again about what our relationship was about. Why did she break off our contact after two years of intense acquaintance? She couldn't answer, just immediately fell into anger and started arguing with me. Over time, I can see that she was another person that I attracted, who wasn't really for me. After that conversation, we returned to our original friendship, but it didn't last long.

After a while, her boyfriend went to prison, and she called me asking for money. She didn't want to borrow; she wanted to sell me her car. I said okay, that we'd draw up a contract, and I'd buy the car, but since I didn't have a driver's license, she could still drive it. I just had to let her know if I needed it.

Another strange situation was when I made an appointment with her for hair extensions, and she postponed it numerous times. Eventually, it was delayed by about four weeks. One day, she didn't even inform me that she wouldn't make it, later saying that she got stuck in such a traffic jam that she finally gave up on visiting me but forgot to tell me. Finally, I called her and said that if she didn't want to do my hair, she could just say so, and I would arrange it elsewhere because I didn't want to wait any longer. In response, she blocked me everywhere and then brought my car to my apartment. She left in it the hair I had paid for, a portion of the money she owed me, and that was the last I saw of her.

I had been forcing myself into similar relationships, which was an automatic behavior for me. Fortunately, only until a certain time. Eventually, I began to realize what was happening, and most of these acquaintances never gave me anything beyond momentary forgetfulness and pain. Most of them died a natural death, but many stayed with me to this day. Fortunately, only in memories.

One of the hardest things I had to realize was that all these adult years, I was looking for people who hurt me the same way as those from my childhood. It was hard for me to admit that my childhood was bad, but when the responsibility for my life fell on me, I still kept hurting myself. My relationships and friendships were toxic and destructive. Alcoholism, drugs, and other substances, as well as psychological and physical violence, were my daily life. I only knew unhappy women who were critical and neglected themselves. I didn't respect money, spending it on another jacket that was only different in color from the previous ones. Unconsciously, I repeated the behaviors of my father, mother, and Helena, plunging into a world from which I should have run away as quickly as possible. I didn't believe in myself, only in others. Always. I lived in all this for a very long time, and understanding it was the most important and at the same time the most difficult step to take.

Today, when I look back at my past acquaintances, I see a lot of valuable lessons. Valuable, but very hard. When in recent months I cleared my surroundings of unsupportive people and those who were toxic to me, I made room for completely different people who now give me the perfect energy for development, not for inflicting more blows on myself. When I started taking care of my health and well-being, my world changed, becoming a much friendlier place on Earth.

Curiosity

In all clubs, including Kult, some of the guests were high on drugs. Perhaps they thought that in such places, drugs were everywhere, which was not true. At some point, when I realized that clients were looking for not only the closeness of dancers, music, and alcohol but also drugs, I began to see this as a good business. I had access to various drugs, but I didn't have anyone who could quickly and discreetly deliver them to me if needed. So, I started carrying ibuprofen with me. These pills were useful when a client needed a fix from me. I would crush them and put them in little bags. In private rooms, where there were no cameras, selling such bags was a very popular way to make good, additional money. Selling real drugs was completely unprofitable and difficult to organize, so clients never got real doses. When someone wanted a boost, I would go to the locker room and prepare a package for him. Sometimes I packed the powder in foil, sometimes in a bag, and sometimes even in cigarette foil.

Touch

The second club in Gdansk which I ended up in became a place where I felt good. I didn't find the usual envy, unhealthy gossiping, and energy-draining sabotage there. I finally found a group of girls who knew how to work together and create somewhat healthier relationships. Of course, it's hard to talk about lifelong friendships and complete trust here because life and work in the club were based on a set of rules, but here you could breathe.

I met a great manager who, despite knowing about my situation from the first club in Gdansk, gave me a chance and didn't look down on me more than the other girls. The club was large and spacious, and every corner was well thought out. So, I have very fond memories of both the team and the club itself. On the first night, a client spent twenty thousand zloty on me, so I had a great start.

I had nothing to complain about. There was no tolerance for bullying, weird venting, or mobbing. My opinion and I were simply respected, we supported each other, and we earned great money. An example was how we treated new dancers. None of us were mean to them but simply helped them integrate into our little world. We helped them understand how it worked and what to do to earn as much as possible. And clients loved, and probably still love, new dancers. Why? Because in their eyes, these were women still untainted by this world, not saturated with cunning.

The girls respected each other and treated each other really well. We helped each other in making more revenue, often by inflating the so-called roses. This involved deceiving the client after paying for champagne that the transaction didn't go through and that he should try again or use a different card. Then a rose in the form of a present was added to the table. In such a situation, when a client bought Cristal champagne for twenty thousand zloty, he ultimately paid forty thousand zloty. When they were Norwegians or Swedes, we would say the champagne cost twenty thousand kronor, and that also worked.

Other situations, like when a client didn't want to pay, make me smile at the memory. In those moments, one of the girls would come with a dustpan and brush and start bustling around the client's feet. When he asked what she was sweeping, he'd hear, "Your straw from your shoes." One day, a German appeared who didn't want to pay. We then used what we called a freebie. It was two, maybe three minutes of private dancing. After this time, he had to either pay or leave. He didn't want to pay even in such a situation. When he started yelling at us and being verbally aggressive, a colleague covered the camera, and I took care of him. I kicked him with my glass shoes so hard that he left with a body densely covered in bruises. I risked a huge fine, maybe even more, but that situation was exceptional. We were not going to let anyone treat us like that. I was always very patient, but that was too much.

The great support of the group helped us earn really big money. There was no pressure or sick competition; we just felt like we were working together.

In Krakow, where I followed my favorite manager, it was a bit harder because those girls had to be taught such cooperation.

Anyway, that second club in Gdansk, Touch, is the one I remember the best of all, and it will stay with me. Even though we later argued over a few not-necessarily important things. I don't keep in touch with all the girls, those relationships died a natural death. I was changing, moving away from alcohol and other substances, and we simply started lacking common topics.

I only remember the end badly, which I'll mention right away. Namely,

Monika, the manager, went on vacation at some point and then didn't come back to us. She moved to Krakow and started working in another club there. So when the new manager Liza came to our club, my career there ended very quickly. Liza was a dancer from my previous club and she didn't grasp reality. On the second night with her, I took a colleague out for leaflets and said that I wasn't coming back to the club, that I was moving to Krakow because I already knew that I wanted and could work only with a manager like Monika. With Monika, I controlled my drinking.

I didn't get drunk so often and so heavily, and I felt very good about it. I told the girl I went out with to come with me to the club where Monika worked. That night we didn't return to the club, and the next day Liza called me. I didn't answer, just texted her that I wasn't coming back to the club and that she shouldn't contact me anymore. She only replied that she blocked my transfer to Krakow with the management. Fortunately, she didn't have that much influence. We called the management, and it turned out that we were allowed to move to Krakow. The only condition was that for two days, or rather nights, we had to commute to Sopot. That was quite cool; we even made a nice profit, about thirty thousand zloty. Then we had two days off to pack, sort out all our affairs, and travel to Krakow.

In Krakow

In Krakow, we were warmly welcomed right away, thankfully Monika was still in a managerial position. Things were really okay, but for the first two weeks, I had a significant problem with earning any money. It was difficult to find a paying client, or problems arose when it came to payment, and the client's card just wouldn't go through. In such cases, we usually went with the client to an ATM or their apartment to get additional cash.

I remember a client with a gold card. Unfortunately, the card had limits, but he told us he had another one. We went to his apartment, and it turned out his wife and child were there. He politely took the card and returned with us to the club to continue having fun.

Another example was when Monika would send me to private rooms to boost the bill a bit, and when I entered, either the meeting was just ending, or I caught the finalization of payment. This was happening constantly, and I didn't understand what was going on, as this had never happened to me before. Of course, there are random situations, and you shouldn't be surprised by them. However, they don't happen that often and don't last that long.

Monika and I wondered what was going on until I finally said that Liza from Gdansk must have cursed me. I couldn't explain it in any logical way. I decided to go for a cleansing with a fortune teller. I don't remember, but I think it was with white sage.

I always believed in magic. I would ground myself in the forest, hug trees, and have a natural connection with all of it. Among dancers, most, if not all, of us believed in the same thing. Spells and cleansing were obvious to us and part of our daily life. The second night after the cleansing at the fortune teller, a very nice client came to my shift. He was German, lived in Australia, and ran his businesses both there and across Europe. I don't remember exactly what he did, but in any case, it brought him a lot of money. His first wife was Polish, so he spoke Polish quite well, though English was better for him. It was really nice, we got along great. He had several gold cards. He bought champagne for two thousand, and I'll just mention that each subsequent one cost about twice as much, up to a limit of twenty thousand zloty. The most expensive champagne came to our table several times. It was one of my best sales nights, and we sat with him for several hours.

After he bought that first twenty-thousand zloty champagne, I called a waitress to invite another girl to the room. I didn't care who, because I was drunk with the happiness that I was earning. Madzia sent Tina to me. I wasn't fond of her, but at that moment, it didn't matter. The cooperation went smoothly, and she did what I asked her to do.

At Kult, every fifty thousand zloty, the client had to sign a statement acknowledging the amounts they were spending. The manager would go to the office, take the form, and then give it to the client to sign. In front of the camera, they would show us their ID, from which we copied the necessary data. This was an effective way to prevent clients from claiming they were unaware of their expenditures due to alcohol or that we were trying to extract information from them. Everything had to be visible on camera, so in case of any disputes, we could rely on facts, not assumptions.

In Krakow, too, there were really nice girls, but I didn't have as good a relationship with them as with the group in Gdansk. They weren't as trained in cooperation, but as I mentioned, it was quite good. It was only after Monika arrived that they began to work on this and gradually, we started to see the first results. Unfortunately, the girl who came there with me experienced some kind of crisis, because after about two or three weeks, she had a big argument with Monika and left Krakow, simultaneously ending her career in this network of clubs. When you leave clubs in such a way, you pay penalties, and the previous earnings are not paid out, you simply end up without any money. When she reached out to the bosses to somehow recover it, she was told it wasn't possible, and then she sent them an email with blackmail. She threatened that if they didn't return her money, she would go to every newspaper and do everything to blow up what happens behind the scenes of the operations of the club. And then they returned her the outstanding money. It was a very interesting case where a dancer got what she wanted. Usually, those who sued would receive their back pay, but in installments of fifty zloty a month. But she fairly quickly and effectively managed to recover the entire debt, ending the problem in a neat, concrete way. I don't know of any other such case, so it stuck in my memory.

Working with a Client

Working with each client looks a little different. One day, an exceptionally generous man appeared, whom I mentioned in the story about the cleansing with the fortune teller. On his first visit, he spent about two hundred thousand zloty and then kept coming back due to a specific situation in his life. He was getting divorced for the second time and made it clear to us from the beginning that he needed to spend his money because he didn't want to share it during the process. At first, we were skeptical because many clients tell us they have a lot of money and it doesn't translate into their bills. But in this case, we quickly understood he was telling the truth.

When the client ordered Cristal or Perrier champagne, he paid twenty thousand zloty for it. A waitress would come in, and I would charge him at the terminal. I would say there was some error and that it had to be charged again. The waitress would go out for a second terminal to make it look more credible and return with a bouquet of artificial roses. We charged the same amount at the terminal, but the receipt was for roses.

Issuing subsequent receipts for roses and continuously bringing them to the room meant that everything was accounted for. Ordering flowers, drinks, and champagne for dancers was the norm in strip clubs, even if it happened every few minutes.

So, each time the client effectively paid twice. We would do such transactions about every twenty minutes unless the central office let us know it was too frequent. We also stopped when the client was too drunk. Then we would let him sleep for about an hour and then return to him.

This particular client bought several bottles of champagne just for me, then also for Tina, a colleague who was working with me at the time. I remember he gave us massages, and we then performed a show for him. He wasn't interested in anything erotic. He came to have a good time and spend as much money as possible in the shortest time. And all this happened after my cleansing ritual at the fortune teller's, after which I felt really good. Some may say it's a coincidence and one thing has nothing to do with the other, but I know and feel my own. I have no doubt that the meeting with the fortune teller helped me get rid of the bad energy invited by a soul that was not favorable to me.

In the club in Krakow, there was a day shift and a night shift. I worked the night shift, so the next day I showed up for work at 10 PM. Right at the entrance, the manager told me that my client from the previous day was in the club. He was currently spending money on the girls from the day shift, but when he saw me, he smiled broadly:

"Oh, my princess is here!"

I then apologized to those girls and took over. I wanted to approach him, sit on his lap, and hug him, but one of the girls stopped me, saying that he wouldn't spend anything on me because he was in love with her. I just replied, "We'll see about that." I did what I wanted and started talking to him. Between the girls, we used Polish, but I spoke English with him. I asked him how he slept, how he spent his time, and if he felt good, affectionately calling him "Honey." I wanted him to feel comfortable. After we talked for a while, he looked at all the girls around and, still holding me on his lap, told them that they could go, as he was now busy and from that moment on, he would only spend money on Anastazja, which was my name in that club. That night he spent about fifty thousand zloty, as the central office forbade us to charge him more. They were afraid that since the client was using our services two days in a row, we would later have a problem with him having spent so much money on us. He never appeared in our club again. He wanted to get rid of his money, so I suspect he went somewhere where he could do it freely.

That night I also had fun with him. Tina and I made good money in a pleasant way. For four hours, we spent time as creatively as the previous night. I taught him to play cards, read his palm, and just played with time and my ideas so he would simply want to be there with us.

There was also another client whom I remember fondly. A young blond guy from the United States. He sat with me at the table for about three and a half hours and spent around forty thousand zloty. It was a weekday and spending time with him at least meant that I would earn a few thousand. Usually, during the week, when a client with more cash showed up, the manager would pull me from the private room and send another girl there, so I had a chance to earn a bit more. Besides, I was her dark horse. When a client had a gold card and wanted to leave for some reason, she often called me to salvage the situation. I could be persuasive. Usually, after talking to me, the client stayed, but sometimes, when he got nervous about having spent too much money or if a dancer was unpleasant to him, he went home anyway. These weren't common situations, but they did happen.

The blond guy was an Eminem fan and even resembled him a bit. During all the time spent with him, that was essentially the main topic of conversation. We danced for him a bit, even rapped a little, and in between, we talked about our interests, dreams, and plans. He bought cheaper champagne and kept asking when there would be sex. In Kult, there was a rule that we couldn't suggest to clients that there would be any intimacy. The clubs didn't provide sexual services, but we whispered in his ear that it would be soon, just pay for one more thing.

Generally, we couldn't tell any client that one of the services was sex. That would have been blatant deception, and it was forbidden. However, it wasn't beneficial to outright say that sex was off the table, so my way was to communicate with a knowing look, a wink, or a half-smile. All of this was to not refuse him outright, to give him a bit of hope, but without any straightforward confirmation from me.

Kult was a chain of clubs owned by Karol Nowakowski, where the same rules applied. In each of them, you could deceive in the same way. When a client had potential, we called him a "Son of Sacrifice." When such a client entered the club, and the manager asked me if he looked like one, I would size him up from head to toe, assessing his shoes, face, state he was in, and the overall impression he made. If everything matched up, I would say yes, I could take him on and get to work. To the first drink of the "Son of Sacrifice," a shot of vodka was added to quickly get him drunk. Usually, after such a move, the client became merry, and his self-control took a back seat. Sometimes it happened that he fell asleep, but we included that in the risk of the whole operation. The second method for bigger earnings was roses. The third was giving clients the wrong currency, so they would spend, for example, crowns more freely. Norwegians and Swedes were like wild animals because the restrictions in their countries affected them quite a bit daily. Attention from Polish women, walking hand in hand to the ATM, smiles, and admiration they received from us were so different from the behavior of their women that they went wild. The more attention they got from us, the more they were committed to spending money. Simple calculation.

Another way to make a client spend as much money as possible was to invite a second girl to the table. If he had previously ordered champagne to the table, in such a situation he would have ordered a second champagne. It was also easier to make a transaction with a rose when one of the dancers occupied the client with something. The cheapest champagne was called Astii and always gave me heartburn the next day. I didn't like it. I liked Perrier the most, Cristal not so much.

The police search

In Krakow, I also had the dubious pleasure of being searched by the police. We were visited by twenty policemen, who were assisted by dogs. They didn't have much to do with us, as all the girls were scantily dressed, and more intimate searching had to be supported by a specific reason and, of course, a warrant.

The search was probably meant to scare us and happened after all the dancers from a shift in Gdansk were detained. They wanted to check if we would start admitting to various things. They asked us how long we had been working and if we had drugs. Whether we took them, whether we were forced into anything, whether we felt good working in such a way, and whether we had families. Even if any of us had something to hide, none of us admitted to anything. A corporate lawyer also appeared quite quickly in Gdansk.

My search was relatively calm. A policewoman asked a colleague to take off her underwear. She categorically refused in a rather dismissive tone, saying there was no way she would do that. We didn't even take off our underwear in private rooms when a client was paying. The policewoman wasn't paying, so there was nothing to discuss. We all spoke up then, saying that she shouldn't even come near us, as we also weren't going to do it. We said we could all undress and stay in just our underwear and line up together. She got flustered, and it didn't come to that. They told us to leave the changing room and go to the private rooms, and they searched all our things. They dumped everything out of the lockers onto the floor so the dogs could sniff around properly. Fortunately, none of us had anything on us at that time. Sometimes one of us would have remnants of marijuana in a bag, so we were quite stressed. In the end, I asked the girls a bit loudly if any of them had accidentally crushed ibuprofen, which we sold to clients as amphetamine, lightening the mood a bit.

Such comments were not unusual for us. We felt untouchable, and often the police would laugh at these jokes with us.

Generally, the police were unpleasant to us. We were annoyed by the throwing around of our things, underwear on the floor, and the general chaos. The unpleasant situation continued behind the bar, where they counted bottles of champagne and money. They checked and asked why some vodkas were open. I suspect they wanted to show their superiority and that they knew perfectly well we were adding stronger drinks to the beer. I have no idea what the search was about, but it's a situation that is deeply ingrained in my memory.

End of Cooperation

Sometimes staying in a place where you don't feel good is stronger than taking sensible action. To leave such a place often requires an impulse. A concrete, eye-opening situation, and then following the voice of intuition. Otherwise, the daily routine and toxicity of relationships gradually undermine our reality and make taking the next steps difficult, or even impossible.

The direct reason for ending my cooperation with the club in Krakow was a situation where I was penalized for feeling ill. I remember visiting do-

ctors and experiencing intense pain in my ovaries. I couldn't walk properly, let alone dance. I reported this to the manager, adding that I got a medical leave. After three or four days, I could return, and then I found out
that I received a significant penalty of four and a half thousand zloty for
the time of my absence. That was too much for me.

When I ended my work as a dancer in Krakow, I reached out to my ex in
England, Daniel. First, I went there for a week, and then for just under four
weeks. Nathaniel was under my mother's care at the time, and I wanted to
see how I would feel in England. This scenario seemed the most sensible
to me at the time, and since my sister was living with my mother, I felt my
son would be safe there.

I wanted to find out if I could earn well and live comfortably in England. My plan was to take Nathaniel and move there, as I no longer had
anything holding me back in Poland.

So I went to England, but not everything went according to my plans.
I was twenty-five years old and wanted to check if Daniel still had a problem with alcohol. We rented a room in Leicester. He was working in a
Polish restaurant, and I was working in clubs – first in Leicester, then in
Birmingham. First and foremost, I didn't like the club where I worked or
the work system. I found myself in the smallest club you could imagine.
There was a stage at the entrance, a small bar, and tiny booths. Cigarettes
were smoked outside, and I remember it being very cold. There, I only got
paid for the drinks purchased by clients if their number matched the number of dances I performed, which I learned after the fact.

*Clubs in England operate completely differently than those in Poland and
Germany. It's a completely different world. In England, clubs charge
what's called a fee just for working there. These are very different amounts
and it works in such a way that you go to work, pay, and whatever you
earn is yours. You keep all the money from private dances, and a much
larger percentage from drinks than elsewhere. There are a lot of girls in
such clubs, but not everyone can earn. If you have to pay just to enter,
sometimes it's hard for them to make enough money to have anything left*

over. I only worked in this type of club once. The second system, which you could find in a large part of clubs, was that at the end of the shift, the dancer gave a specific percentage of her earnings to the owners.

The first night I had four private dances, which gave me a net earning of eighty pounds. My living expenses were really low, so I concluded that it was really bad for the first night. The second night, a client who bought us fifteen drinks each appeared. One drink was about ten pounds for me. Simple calculations meant that for that many drinks, I should have gotten at least one hundred and fifty pounds, but I got nothing. I sat with the guy for about five hours, during which he kept going out for a smoke, to the bathroom, for a line, to the ATM, or God knows what else. When he left and my shift was over, I went to get my earned money and was told that since I hadn't danced, I wasn't owed any payment. That was my last night in that club.

I smoothly moved to the next club, this time in Birmingham, where I initially went for four days. The accommodation was free, but I felt so bad there that I only lasted three nights. There was a Polish guy at the door, and I also met one of the club's stars. Maybe I couldn't blend into the atmosphere of those particular places anymore. That was the time when I gave up on clubs.

For the rest of the planned four weeks in England, I worked in a restaurant with my ex, Daniel. During this short stay, we argued a few times so intensely that I ended up using drugs to relieve the stress. I also missed Nathaniel terribly. Unfortunately, or perhaps fortunately in retrospect, drugs made me look and feel really bad the next day. Not only was it not entirely good while taking them, but the subsequent comedowns caused me to completely detach from reality. A swollen face, vacant look, headache, and complete powerlessness were the price for literally a moment of elevation after taking those substances. Overwhelmed by this, as well as his return to drinking, I quickly returned to Poland. I realized that I needed to earn money for expenses quickly and that the worst thing I could do was return to my ex and the world I was slowly escaping from.

The Hypocrisy of the Girls

A popular boxer often came to the club in Sopot, and each time his state indicated the consumption of a fairly large dose of drugs. While we had been in that world long enough and knew the effects of specific drugs, in his case, we couldn't determine what he was taking. Each time his gaze, strange movements, and behavior led us to guess that he was in some specific mix. Whenever he left, we girls would always discuss it.

When I was at the Pink Sphinx to typically drink green celery juice, and he happened to be in the bar, he always called me to his table and asked the waitress to bring me the most expensive champagne. The second time I met him in another restaurant, he ordered the place closed because there would be a private party. Each time he saw me or any dancer, he behaved similarly, as if every place belonged to him. Sometimes he was alone, often with people who didn't seem like his usual company. This was when there was a lot of talk about his domestic situation. Supposedly he was beating his wife, but what the truth was, nobody knows.

Another famous person was an actor who not only came to the club as a client but also had encounters with one of the dancers. It was more of a casual sexual relationship than a real relationship. I know this famous actor and the owner of the Essence Club were good friends, so the owner quickly found out about this situation. He didn't have a very good opinion of Daria (that was her name) because she quickly ended up in bed with newly met men. In this case, Szur was a club client, and that already caused a specific conflict. An erotic dancer is not a prostitute, but here it unfortunately turned out to be the same.

Daria had been working there for quite a long time. She was really pretty in the face, though her body left much to be desired. Manager Kamil was very biased toward her, and it was during his shift that the situation with Szur began, or rather the start of that situation. I remember she got very upset when I danced to a song by a popular Polish rapper. She wanted to be the only girl in the club who danced to his music. She claimed that song was already in her dance repertoire, so I couldn't use it. It was quite funny, but I simply replied that I would choose a different repertoire and wouldn't cause her any trouble. The club was still closed at the time and there was no music as such, and the girls were getting dressed. So, I approached the DJ and, wanting to mock Daria, loudly asked why he hadn't warned me that some songs were reserved in this club, especially that particular one. I said this in a rather amused tone, but I already knew that this had ruined my relationship with her. It didn't bother me in the slightest, and the whole situation was mostly just funny to me. After this and similar situations, you could quickly tell which girls were very insecure. In this case, the older dancer felt threatened by the new one who, in her eyes, was not only younger but also slimmer. And prettier. So, she felt threatened and couldn't handle it.

There were more such situations. For example, I would approach a table and before I could blink, she would join the client I was talking to and continue the conversation. I would just smile and walk away, but when our eyes met, I could see anger in hers. In this club, card payments were only made at the bar because that's where the terminal was connected. Sometimes, when I approached the bar so a client could pay for champagne, she would come up to me and nudge me in such a way that I dropped the terminal. It was strange, and I didn't fully understand if that was her intention. One day, she was less lucky. I remember several of us girls were drunk and since it was quiet, we took a nap. At one point, the boss came in, shouting and waking us all up. Daria wanted to say something, but the boss, probably having heard and seen how she had treated me before, responded quite bluntly:

"You just shut up. New, young girls are coming in, and instead of supporting them, you act like some princess. You're not a dancer from a celebrity event to feel like the only one here. There are no fights over songs, no reserving of tracks, what is this even supposed to be? If such a situation happens again, it won't be so nice."

And apparently did it well, as there was constant news about his new purchases. He was ugly but wealthy. He had a new house and would pick her up from the club in his new car, which made her feel over the moon. One day, Daria burst into the changing room full of euphoria, shouting that she was going to live with her new boyfriend, that she would now live in a big house and could invite her friends over. Then one of the colleagues, Blanka, responded that it was wonderful, that she had nothing to worry about, and that now everything would be really good.

Just before, I had talked to Blanka about Daniel, as I had recently moved in with him. She told me that moving in with him was not a very good idea, as it could create only trouble.

I was almost taken aback, and my head swirled. I thought, wow, how fake and vain this world is! My relationship with Daniel, who was a chef, had been going on for some time and was viewed by these girls as being fraught with eternal problems. And Daria's relationship with a guy she knew for a week, who smuggled drugs and wasn't exactly likable, is wonderful? It didn't make sense and shook my view of the world. A normal guy with emerging problems is unacceptable, but a guy who lives off problems is something desirable?

A few days later, she came to work and she was very upset. I don't know if she even registered that I was also in the changing room. She said that there had been a party at home, alcohol was flowing, and drugs were one of the snacks. Her boyfriend got so high that he was almost unreachable. In the morning, he was supposed to take her to the hospital for a minor procedure, but of course, he couldn't. Crying, she said she felt that it couldn't be it. She lived with him for maybe four days.

I then noticed a big difference between me and Daria. I didn't care about money when it came to relationships. I paid for Daniel's rehab, I managed on my own. I just wanted to be loved. And she moved in with her new fling and at the first foreseeable situation in that world, she just took her things and left him. She didn't look back at any feelings, attachment, or tender-

ness between them. The first situation, which she could have resolved, even by taking a taxi on his money, made her simply forget the relationship and great love. I couldn't understand it.

At the party Daria mentioned, there were dancers from our club. However, Daria went to bed earlier because she had to be at the hospital early the next morning. It ended up with her not speaking to everyone for several days, squarely blaming all the invited guests for what happened. None of the girls wanted to approach her first, as they simply didn't feel guilty about the whole situation.

I then saw how my world was different from the one Daria and perhaps other girls from the club lived in. I was at work. I was a dancer from 8 PM to 4 or 6 AM and then I went home, to my own life. I could separate the two without any problem. I didn't create unnecessary connections, and what I did at work did not significantly penetrate my daily life. This was natural for me and allowed me to maintain some kind of inner balance. It wasn't always easy, but this system worked for me, and I stuck to it. What Daria did was destructive for her and for many others, and it couldn't serve her well, even for a short time. I also remember my ritual of shaking my head in a specific way when I entered the club. It was a symbolic change of persona. I stepped into my role, which I then left at the club. The bouncers knew this move of mine and would always mimic it from afar when they saw me. It was great because it gave me a positive vibe right at the entrance, which helped me get through my shift in a much better mood. I couldn't understand why other dancers remained in their roles even outside the club. Why? Perhaps they liked that atmosphere, and it was more than just a job for them, but I dare say they might not have been able to separate it from themselves. For them, it was mostly about the money. But that world didn't consume me. I felt so different from them. Alone.

And today, I am proud that I didn't become too absorbed in it all.

In Bavaria

When I returned from England to Krakow, it turned out that there was no work for me. Every attempt to get a job in a club ended in failure for me. Most clubs didn't want girls from Kult because of its rules. After two or almost three weeks, I had to decide what to do next and ended up deciding to go abroad.

I remember posting on a Facebook group while looking for work, and that's where the owner of a club in Bavaria spotted me. I agreed to go, thinking that I would see what it was like to work in Germany; I would earn some money and could return to Poland to decide what to do next. I was not disappointed. I traveled from Poland to Bavaria by bus, and the owner picked me up upon arrival. After the trip, he behaved like a gentleman and took me and another girl from Slovakia, who had also come to work, out for lunch. He was okay, though sometimes he was a bit overbearing. However, he always tried to make sure each of us was satisfied. The girls supported each other, and interesting relationships formed. I felt peaceful there. When I got drunk or felt tired, he let me go home. There were also a few clients who left substantial money. One evening I managed to earn about two thousand euros. The only thing I couldn't stand there was the mess. Unfortunately, the owner hadn't thought to hire a cleaner and only counted on the dancers occasionally taking care of tidying up the space, which wasn't obvious to them.

I rested in that place and earned a lot of money, which allowed me to breathe a bit easier. If I were to recommend clubs, it would be those in smaller German towns, because there, besides money, there is also a chance for peace.

The girls in the club generally had trouble earning. For various reasons, including external ones. I remember one of them was really pretty, but due to her very short stature, she didn't have too many clients. Another in the group, slim and attractive, unfortunately, drank too much and it was evident that she was very tired of this job. Usually, when she started drinking, she would end the evening drunk. My experience and confidence in what I was doing allowed me to earn well in various situations and with different clients.

The apartment for the dancers was located above the club. When I got up early, I liked to cook and often served the girls whatever I was making. I also prepared meals for myself for several days, which gave me more time to rest, something I made use of. I enjoyed going for walks in the forests, near the water. It calmed me down, and that's when I think I started to meditate. The environment allowed me to recharge my batteries, and that in turn gave me a somewhat different outlook on the future. I felt well-adjusted to life and the world.

In Munich

Munich was not a good place for me. I also don't have fond memories of working with the agent I collaborated with there. His name was Lukas.

At that time, you could find work as a dancer either by yourself or through an agency. To use such a company's services, you had to contact them and go through some formalities. Information about age, experience, dimensions, or weight was important. After filling out the paperwork, it was essential to take pictures. Based on these, a profile was created, which later served the agent to quickly submit offers to clubs that were interested in the dancer from his database.

Lukas was probably from Romania, and the cooperation with him initially went well. The only thing was that I had to invest a bit in it. A professional photo session for his website cost about two thousand zloty. This included makeup, hairstyle, and arrangements. Everything looked really good, but only during the session.

The first sign that I shouldn't have gone there was my mistake with the bus departure dates. The driver informed me that I had come to the station a day too early when he was checking my ticket. This was very strange to me because I had bought the ticket about two weeks earlier. Had I not looked at the date even once during that time? Besides, I was always very organized, so getting the date wrong was shocking to me. I wasn't quite sure what to do at that moment. The first thing I did was call the agent to tell him I would be one day late. He said it was nothing to worry about, that the work was supposed to be on the weekend, and it was still a week away, so I shouldn't worry. I had come to the station from the other end of Krakow, so not wanting to lug my suitcase with me, I left it in a locked station locker. I came to the station with the girls from the club because they wanted to see me off. When I realized the situation with the ticket, I quickly changed plans and went with them to karaoke. Then I spent the night at their apartment, took a shower, and got ready for the next day. When I arrived in Munich, I was picked up by a driver whose behavior should have immediately alarmed me.

"You look completely different than in the pictures."

"How did you recognize me then?"

He seemed flustered and didn't quite know how to answer, but the situation was at least strange for me. He tensed up and I didn't entirely trust him getting into the car with him. I asked him to drive carefully, and he just reassured me, saying that everything was okay.

His statement that I didn't look like my pictures stayed with me, and I felt slightly uneasy. So I prepared myself well. I applied face masks, beautiful makeup, and a sexy dress, and went to the club.

At the bar stood the boss's girlfriend, completely transformed from head to toe. She probably was from Vietnam. All the new girls who arrived first went to her for a short training. She explained what needed to be done and moved on to the next new girl. That day three of us were new, and she first called me over. I approached the bar and started in English:

"Hi, I'm Anastazja from Poland, from Lukas's agency."

She didn't respond, just kept rummaging through papers under the bar. This went on for about two or three minutes, so I walked away, thinking

I'd come back when she emerged from the bar. Just as I took two steps, I heard her voice behind me. We spoke in English:

"Where are you going?"

"I thought you were busy, so I was going to sit over there and wait for a moment when you're available for me."

"But I didn't say you could leave."

"You didn't even respond to my hello, so I didn't want to distract you from your work, and I decided to sit down."

"No, wait until I'm finished."

"No, I'll sit and wait until you're done with whatever you're doing."

"But I was supposed to show you around the club now."

"Then do that."

She started showing me around and explaining the rules for selling champagne and others, which were the same as in other clubs. To everything she said, I responded with "I know," just like in Poland, when you indicate during a conversation that you understand what's being said. However, my constant affirmations seemed to irritate her so much that she said I was in her club now and asked me what my constant "I know" even meant. I told her I had been a dancer for several years, I knew how it worked, and to confirm that one understands what the other person is talking about is normal in Poland. I also added that I was supposed to have a male boss, not a boss lady, but maybe I had heard wrong.

"Well, you're not in Poland now, you're here."

"Yes, but that doesn't change the fact that it's my habit to respond that way when I already know something."

She then took it as a huge offense. She snapped that I think I know everything. I replied that yes, I know how to entice customers to buy champagne and other drinks, and that's what I was affirming. I don't know, however, anything about the layout of private rooms and things related to the location of specific things in this club. She snorted at me and walked away.

During my first shift, I sold a few bottles of champagne, and around 1 AM, I went to the changing room to smoke. I took out my phone and saw a message from Lukas saying that I couldn't stay in this club because I looked different than in the pictures. I immediately sensed it wasn't about that. So I asked if this was a way to get rid of more experienced girls from the club who didn't fit in with the local bartender. After all, he had seen me several times in person, we had talked, and he had no complaints. He replied that I didn't know who I had crossed and that I had to end my work there. So my adventure in Munich started and ended quite quickly, lasting just one weekend. Later, when I met many girls abroad, most of them complained about this particular club in Munich. So, it was good that it ended that way, and I didn't stay longer, losing nerves, money, and time.

That same night, two girls from Lithuania, who supposedly also looked different than in the pictures, received a similar message.
We all worked there for a few days, and then they went to the Czech Republic, while I was transferred to another club.

Back then, I was already on the path of self-development and knew that I had no control over what came my way, but I did have control over how I received it, how I reacted, and whether I took it to heart. It wasn't entirely clear to me yet, but I already had some knowledge on the subject. Various situations happened in my life, and I could, as I do now, draw conclusions from them and move forward.

Lena, the girl who introduced me to that agent, was supposed to join me at the club. However, when she found out I was no longer there, she called Lukas and told him that she wouldn't go to that club either. Initially, he protested, saying what kind of favoritism this was, but after a heated exchange of words, he agreed to what she wanted. Generally, his approach was that if a girl worked with him, she should do whatever he wanted. He was wrong in our case, as neither Lena nor I wanted to be money-making robots. It was our way of life; we had to adhere to some rules, but it was our life, and our rules also had to be respected in some way. We didn't want to stay with other workers in Lukas's villa, as there was a non-stop party, with many girls, and it was hard to talk about normal living conditions. So, he got a bit tired with us, but he arranged a place for us in an apartment for dancers for twenty euros a day, and we could continue our cooperation. I still argued with him about the photos and my resemblance to them, but the topic was not as heated as before and gradually faded into history. The result of our discussions was that when he came to the club where we worked, he just greeted us and talked normally with the rest of the team.

Given the uncertain situation with Lukas, we didn't want to stick only to the work he provided, plus there was no such thing as exclusivity with the agency we had signed with. So, in the meantime, we went to work at another club without telling Lukas. The owner of that club provided us with accommodation he rented out to workers, and we started our shift. It happened that Lukas showed up there, and when he saw us, a little hell broke loose. He demanded money from us, even though the situation was irrational. Funnily enough, he also wanted money from a girl who was with us, even though her profile wasn't even in his database. Of course, he got no money from us.

In the second club in Munich, still under Lukas's agency, I had a much better experience. I remember it fondly because there were fewer clients, but they were wealthy. You could go out with a client to the ATM for cash. Often, the boss ordered meals for us, sometimes paying for everything himself, other times half. Such daily support for our work was very uplifting. At the bar in the club worked Jana, a very nice girl from the Czech Republic. Besides her, I also befriended a girl from Russia. It was funny because the dancers didn't speak German, and the bar girls didn't speak English, so we spoke to them in Polish, and they responded in Russian. Communication was limited, but it didn't bother us, and we managed very well, continually developing cooperation and building interesting bonds. There were wonderful girls from Romania in the group, and generally, there was a healthy calm in the club. Earlier I mentioned befriending, but those relationships with the team were not really friendships, but an ability for healthy cooperation. When Lukas appeared, those girls who wanted to could vanish into the changing room, and what's more, they were given a heads-up that he was coming.

Eventually, my adventure with Lukas and his agency ended, and I moved on to other clubs. At that time, I thought I had already left the episode of working under his wings behind me. However, I was mistaken.

The continuation of the story happened when someone asked about Lukas on a Facebook group for dancers I was a part of. I didn't hold back and laid out the whole truth. I confirmed my statements with screenshots of conversations as soon as he started denying them. A flurry of comments from other girls who supported me emerged. They included warnings about clubs connected to Lukas, advising others to avoid them due to the challenging conditions and unfair treatment dancers faced there. The situation quieted down, only to flare up again after five or six months while I was working in Hamburg. By then, I had pretty much moved on from it. After some time, I received a message from Lukas on Messenger. Since it landed in my SPAM folder, I wasn't aware of it initially. It turned out there were more messages from Lukas, in which he openly threatened me. He wrote that if I didn't delete all that information, his lawyer would contact me. He recorded messages where he yelled about what he would do to me if I didn't follow his orders and so on. He threatened that if I showed up in Germany, he would harm me. I retorted that I had family in Germany and he couldn't do anything about my stay in the country. He didn't know that I was actually living and working there at the time, and I didn't plan to tell him that. Funnily enough, his partner tried to offer me work, suggesting that I couldn't manage without him. I told him that I could handle things perfectly well on my own and didn't need his help. I asked if he was pretending to be ignorant of the fact that I was managing just fine by myself.

Eventually, I checked the Facebook group and saw that he had added one last comment, but he hadn't tagged me in it, so I hadn't noticed it. It stated that I should stop lying and that the matter would end up in court. He finished his comment with just "Regards, Lukas." So, I responded to that comment by posting everything I had on the matter. I had nothing to hide, so I uploaded more screenshots of conversations, a video from the night at the club, and pictures where I supposedly didn't look like myself.

I added that treating girls in such a way was unthinkable. I was over a thousand kilometers from home. I had left my child with family for three weeks to earn a living, not to play some vile games based on the deceit of unprofessional agents. The fear for my safety, unstable earnings, and a life steeped in lies were completely unnecessary in a world that was already challenging enough. I never retouched photos because a lie has no legs, and my appearance could easily be verified. It was funny and, I believe, completely unnecessary. I got quite carried away while writing my last comments, which led to Lukas being blocked on many such groups. These groups had various connections and stuck together, so the situation I described quickly spread to more people in the industry. This, in turn, made it difficult for Lukas to find dancers for work or collaborate with any club. The world of dancers is relatively small, and it's hard to hide anything that happens in it, especially when it concerns disputes between an agent and dancers from his base. I didn't want it to end this way, as my only intention in the discussion was to clarify that what I was saying was true.

In Hamburg

Later, instead of going to Munich, I started traveling to Hamburg. Practically, it meant leaving Nathaniel with my mother and going to work. A week at work, then returning to my mom for a few days, and then back to work for three weeks. Officially, I was returning to work in Poland, but in reality, I was going to Hamburg. I worked there at the Ala Charm Club.

At first, I liked it for a few days, but then it started to wear on me. It was huge, there were a lot of girls and they were cool, but overall the atmosphere and clientele weren't my cup of tea. I didn't agree with the rules and just didn't like the vibe of the club. There was this so-called Shower Show. You had to go under a shower visible to everyone completely naked and perform an erotic show. This annoyed me because I would straighten my very curly hair for work, which would completely lose its look when wet. This was a real problem because, after such a performance, you had to quickly start looking for clients. And there I was, usually with such messed-up hair, half curly, half straight, no exception, I had to get going too. It was the best, fastest way to earn money. In those moments, I knew that the more drunk a client I found, the more I would earn. So, I would quickly scan the observers and approach where I thought the most susceptible client was. Luckily, I only worked there for three weeks. I didn't make a lot of money there. A girl I worked with told me about another club in Hamburg, similar to Kult, but you could make much bigger transactions there during shifts.

I decided to try the second club recommended by this girl. The boss's girlfriend, Milena, spoke Polish well, but she wasn't there that day and one of the dancers translated for me from English to German. The club owner then said we could start collaborating, but I needed to give him my tax identification number. I was thrilled because it meant a chance to work on a contract. It was a big relief and gave me a sense of security. Handling the paperwork took about a week and a half, and I remember my mom helped me with it. During that time, I was also looking for an apartment, which was tough at that time in Hamburg. Eventually, I found a huge room in a separate part of the house, which was kind of like a separate apartment. A kitchen combined with a living room, a bathroom, and a terrace, so it was okay. I had trouble with registration, so I kept the one I had at my mom's. Dealing with that kind of paperwork was pointless for now.

I started working at the club on a weekend and on my first night, I earned over six hundred euros, which was a decent amount. There, the base pay was given out nightly or once a week, and both the frequency and the amount suited me well. However, the club was in a basement and it was always smoky, and the cleanliness level wasn't too high. Despite that, the atmosphere at the beginning was okay, and I could even cheat the clients a bit, so I stayed there for almost a year. One of the biggest downsides of working there was dealing with the boss's girlfriend. Milena had difficulty accepting other attractive dancers, so my colleague Nadia and I had many tough times with her. Despite this, I was earning a lot and it still made more sense for me to stay there than to look for another place.

The boss, Carsten, resembled a famous Austrian with a mustache. Romka from Poland, equally jealous as Milena, worked at the bar, and among the girls was also Rosa, whom I began to befriend after clearing up a specific situation with a girl from Brazil, with whom I didn't initially get along. The situation with her was quite complicated at first. During conversations, she often flirted with me, which I took as a joke. I enjoyed this game, so I went along with it, but it turned out that what she was doing was an attempt to get closer to me. Rosa was a lesbian, which I didn't know, so I was unwittingly giving her hope for something more. Fortunately, I eventually realized and, not wanting to hurt her, wrote her a sincere letter. She accepted the situation and said that she herself wasn't quite sure what I meant and where exactly we stood. Over time, we became very good friends and it all faded into the past. Our relationship lasted about six years. I have fond memories of her, wish her all the best, and, I hope, she does the same for me.

After a year, I had enough. Milena's behavior, which was increasingly weighing on me, was slowly driving the dancers to their mental limits. At one point, Marlen left. She was a pretty, attractive German and quickly found work elsewhere. When she returned to the club a week later for her things, I stood behind her in the dressing room, patted her on the back, and told her she had made the right decision because everyone needs to look out for themselves as best they can. She just turned to me and smiled, and that's when I noticed that the boss's son was standing near us. I had no idea if he heard anything, but I didn't continue the topic. Sometime later, I met her in town and asked her in detail where she was working and how it was going.

She told me she had a nice boss and a group of girls with whom she could maintain quite healthy relationships. She said she had the chance to perform a nice pole dance, which wasn't possible in Milena's club due to the risk of leg injuries from broken glass from a nearby wall of mirrors – you couldn't take a comfortable swing with your leg if you wanted to keep it intact. And of course, keep the mirrors whole.

Considering what Marlen told me, I talked to Nadia about maybe checking out this club. I wanted to do it unofficially, secretly, without Milena's knowledge, who could make it difficult for us or be even more unpleasant afterward. There was going to be something like a fair or a series of concerts, so we were particularly interested in visiting this place. Moreover, our club was going to be closed that day, so there was nothing stopping us from "scouting the area." We decided we would see how much we could earn and how we would feel there. I remember the moment I entered the club, I immediately said to Nadia that I was staying there. The stage was small, with a spinning pole and beautifully finished interior. Several large private rooms were organized, and dances could also be performed at the bar. The whole place made such a good impression that I had no doubts about wanting to move there. Traditionally, the boss's girlfriend was at the bar, this time a great, excellent, and communicative Wioletta. In addition to her, another girl worked in the same position, a bit before her sixties, whom we called Pipi. We treated her like a mother. She not only stood at the bar but also cleaned there, coming over in between to braid our hair or just fix it and chat. She always asked all of us if everything was okay. We caught a relationship that stayed with us even outside the club. After that one night, I stayed there.

A few days later, I returned to the old club only to take my things and resign. I honestly said that I had had enough of Milena and that's why I was leaving. I explained that the situations she created and escalated were so toxic that it was hard for me to function normally in that club, let alone work and earn satisfying money. The boss and his son asked me to wait because Milena was about to show up, and I had the opportunity to say this in her presence so that they, in turn, could draw some conclusions from it. I agreed and repeated the same thing in front of Milena. She said that it wasn't like that, that I was taking it wrong, and she didn't mean it that way. I then stated that the boss didn't know about many situations, and what she made the girls do and how she treated them was not okay and couldn't be interpreted any other way. The boss turned pale, and the conversation generally showed him a completely different picture of the club he was running.

The club I joined was called Bon Bon, and that was the final chapter of my stripping adventure. Then the pandemic began. After some time, I returned for another two weeks to Ala Charm and made quite a good sum of money. However, the club was shut down because it ceased to bring in the profits the owners desired. This happened in the year two thousand and twenty.

Life is full of lessons, and everything we receive in it has a purpose. Stripping was something I needed, and I don't regret it being a part of my life. Interacting with the dancers and clients who unwound from their lives after hours not only taught me many valuable behaviors and tricks but also helped me find my way. Many situations could have shattered me, pushed me into a corner, either completely assimilating into that world or losing myself beside it. However, things turned out differently.

HEAVEN

OR THE PATH TO HAPPINESS

Introduction to Change

Changing incorrect beliefs about oneself is difficult. If for twenty, or thirty years we are certain that we don't deserve love, safety, and happiness, it's hard to change that in just a few days. Consistency, faith, and determination are the foundation of actions that will eventually lead to change. It's worth dedicating as much time as needed. Time will pass anyway, so why not learn new, healthy beliefs that allow us to live in the world we dream of?

Childhood and working in clubs made me completely lose trust in others and in myself, and this feeling stayed with me for many years. Only at the age of twenty-seven did I begin to wake up from the nightmare and slowly realize how much I had harmed myself with my attitude over those precious years. I didn't respect my thoughts and behaviors, my body, my well-being, or my dreams. I didn't take care of myself, both physically and mentally. For instance, when I had a toothache, I was reluctant to go to the dentist, not allowing myself to think that regular check-ups could have prevented that pain.

The moment that shook me was like an arrow to the heart. It was the time when I was leaving the club in Krakow due to a punishment I received during medical leave. I was informed that I had cancer. In its early stages, which I could still get rid of. It hit me so hard that my entire life flashed before my eyes. I saw all my actual achievements, lack of faith in my own strength, my trivialized successes, shallowness of emotions, and many situations where I simply didn't treat myself as a person worthy of praise and self-love.

Despite many symptoms, cancer was a shock to me. When I finally found out what was wrong, fortunately, it turned out that everything was in the early stages. I was advised to have surgery to remove the tumors near my uterus. I had to do it quickly because the risk of metastasis and tumor growth was high. However, when I went to the hospital for the surgery, the doctors decided that they couldn't just remove the tumors and that the only right decision was to remove the entire uterus. I didn't agree to that. At the same time, I decided to move to Germany permanently to start proper treatment. I did it and quickly found a doctor. We started treatment and in a German hospital, the procedure to remove the tumors was performed. Everything went without complications and it's now just another memory of mine.

When, after resigning from the clubs, I started more down-to-earth jobs, I noticed that women in normal life don't compete with each other as much as in the world of dancers. This was an important lesson for me and it opened my eyes to how I had lived before.

Of course, some women added fuel to the fire, with their sharp tongues, they liked to tease and snip in various situations, but over time I learned to dismiss it with a smile and silence. I understood that those years as a stripper weren't wasted. They were difficult, very valuable lessons for me. This personal success I have today, I danced out for myself. I always felt colorful, beautiful, and full of energy, even when it was covered by a thick layer of daily pain. I was full of internal contradictions, but at that time, working in the clubs was exactly what I needed and what I had to do for myself.

Nathaniel and Jaromir

It's hard to explain to a woman what the love for a child feels like if she isn't or hasn't been a mother. It's a feeling that is born with the child. The same happens when a second child is born. It's hard to imagine a feeling you don't know, right? You may wonder, will I love my child? Will I love my second child as much as I love the first? It's amazing how much love we have inside us, more than we even know. It's uplifting and beautiful. Maybe that's good proof that we can love ourselves, that it's possible, even if we can't yet imagine it.

When my first son was born, I didn't know how I was going to cope; or what it all would look like. But I naively believed everything would be alright. Subconsciously, I felt that I could handle it and it would be fine. I didn't worry about the difficulties I had at the time. That was also the first time I felt responsible for someone by choice. Before that, I had been responsible at various times in my life for my brother, father, mother, and sister. When my son was born, I became a mother and not only had to be responsible for him but also wanted to be. I felt and convinced myself that with him everything would be easier.

My family projected their complexes onto me, making me responsible for their mistakes and life difficulties. For the feelings and memories smoldering inside them that they couldn't express in any other way.

Nathaniel is a special child to me. I know that every mother thinks her child is special, but he came into my life at a time when he managed to do something amazing. Since he appeared, he taught me not only to love him, which came instantly, but also to love myself. Because of him, I started to feel positive about myself, which was completely different from my previous view of reality and the world burning inside me.

I began to learn to take care of myself and my space and to assert my own identity. I started setting boundaries. I remember that I quickly began to feed him with a bottle. For the first month, I breastfed him because my father and his mother told me to (my father had forbidden me to buy formula, claiming that only breastfeeding women are real mothers). Nathaniel cried every night, and I couldn't cope, even though I did everything I could. I then went to a doctor and for the first time heard words I should have heard much earlier. The doctor told me then to listen to no one but to proceed according to what I want and feel, in other words, according to my intuition. Since I hadn't slept for a month, my child was always crying, and I was thinking about buying formula, I should just do it. I should only listen to myself and act as I feel.

I remember that it was a huge revelation for me, and I finally felt permission to follow my intuition. I left the doctor's office and immediately bought formula. I had boiled water in a thermos because I always carried it with me. I made him that formula right away and gave it to him. Nathaniel then fell asleep, and as I walked home on foot for about forty minutes, I was at peace. It was around mid-April. I heard birds, people, the noise of the lake and leaves, and I couldn't believe how peaceful it all was. I then saw the contrast between what my father said and the action I took based on my needs. My father's words caused guilt in me and made my child cry. Acting according to my intuition made my child sleep peacefully. I needed only a few warm, significant words from the doctor to set me on the right path. My child was hungry, and with my chronic stress, I was unable, despite my efforts and love, to give him what he needed. Bottle feeding helped me start to regain balance.

I became pregnant with my second child with more awareness. But for a long time, I thought I was a bad mother. Until the third year of life, my unbaptized son was simply happy, splashing in puddles, dirty, and always running. My family frowned upon this. Only when I cut myself off from them could I let him play freely without angry eyes around, so I allowed him spontaneous, childlike behavior. I finally allowed myself to think that I am a good, sufficient mother.

My Guardian Angel

People can come into our lives for unknown reasons, like so-called Guardian Angels. Sometimes it's a kind neighbor who always remembers to water your plants in your presence and asks for nothing in return, sometimes a friend who always calls right when you need to hear a kind voice, and sometimes a friend who takes in your painful experiences with calmness and strength, which she can impart to you just like that, simply. I was lucky to find someone like that in my life. Although, it would probably be more accurate to say that he found me.

I met Ryszard before my first pregnancy when I was about eighteen years old. I worked in a bar where a man named Ryszard, who seemed to be in his mid-forties, came in. He was a warm, positive person. Unfortunately, he had a problem with alcohol, which I realized during his first visit. After drinking, he reminded me a lot of my father. Ryszard gave me a thousand zlotys that night. He said I was beautiful, that I had beautiful, green eyes. He asked for my phone number, but I didn't give it to him because, first, I didn't want to, and second, because of my situation, I didn't have a cell phone.

Later, Ryszard came to the bar a few more times and after we became friends, I gave him a phone number that I bought with the money he gave me. He could call me several times a day, and usually, I put it on speaker-phone and Ryszard talked. You could say that Ryszard coming into my life was some kind of fate. I believe he was a kind of Guardian Angel who was there to help me at that time. I couldn't keep that job and couldn't find another. Ryszard was a convenient option. He needed someone to listen to him then. He supported me just for that. He paid for my room, cosmetics, and clothes, bought groceries for me, and made me feel very safe at the time. And people found it hard to believe that I wasn't sleeping with him. They found it hard to believe that nothing was going on between us. People told him that if that was the case, he wasn't a real man, and they accused me of using him.

One night, I let my friends do something I know was a huge mistake. When Ryszard was sleeping drunk, I let them rob him. There was a party, some kind of barbecue or something. Someone from my group said they were short of money, and Ryszard had a lot. So, he asked me if he could take some from Ryszard, and I agreed. I couldn't forgive myself for a long time.

The whole relationship with Ryszard taught me to be a good listener, which was very useful to me later when I worked in clubs.

Ryszard loved me very much, but it was a platonic love. Our only physical contact was some occasional hugging or a kiss on the forehead or cheek.

It reminded me of a healthy relationship with a father. I was bothered that he drank, but every day, I was grateful to him for everything he did for me. That he came to see me after work. I was living with my friend at the time, and we would cook for him or bake a cake. He was very happy about it. I know that after a love disappointment with a certain Monika, he never decided to be in a relationship again.

Not long ago, less than a year ago, I found him on FB and wrote to him. I confessed how much I regretted that situation and how grateful I was to him for taking care of me then. I wrote to him that he was my Angel, that he helped me a lot, and if I ever have the chance to help him, he should reach out to me because he can count on me. He replied that he cried when he read the message. He thanked me very much and went back to many situations we had experienced together. When I wrote to him about how my life had turned out, he reminded me that back when we were friends, only he believed in me. Very much so. He always told me that I would go far, but I had to change my company. That I had more sense, that I was worth more than I thought. I remember laughing at that in my mind at the time. And I couldn't believe it because my whole life I had heard the exact opposite.

When I left for Germany while pregnant, I remember Ryszard standing at the bus stop and crying a lot. Later, we didn't have frequent contact. I wrote him letters from time to time, telling him that I wasn't entirely happy, that I was afraid to change anything, to go back and be the black sheep again. I remember writing the second letter, crying after another argument with my father. It was probably about the dinners I prepared. My father yelled at me that I made him the same thing every other day, and I, being pregnant, really wanted spring soup with peas. He said I wasn't a woman because I couldn't cook properly. I replied that if he didn't tell me what he wanted to eat, I would cook for myself. I then went to the park with a piece of paper and wrote a letter. The next day, still under the influence of emotions, I sent it.

Ryszard had my German phone number, and when the letter reached him, about two weeks later, I got a message from him saying that if I trusted him, I could return to Poland and he would help me. With insurance, finding a doctor, and finding a place to live. I didn't go then. I didn't go out of fear. At that time, I was serving, and even though my little Nathaniel didn't sleep during the day or at night, I cleaned, cooked, managed, and cooked. I often left my room because I couldn't manage. And I even got scolded for that.

But in the end, I couldn't take it anymore, I realized I had somewhere to go back to, and I wrote to Ryszard. And then everything went quickly. I arrived by train in Gdynia and he was there waiting for me at four in the morning. When he saw me with a stroller and a small suitcase, he started to cry. At that moment, I was happy and free. I wasn't being told anymore that I was insufficient in almost every field.

Why didn't I do this earlier? How far had I gone into the patterns of my childhood and how much did I feel that I had to live the only way I knew? How hard was it for me to believe that I could live a different way...

Therapy

Over time, I understood that getting rid of the fear inside me was my only way out. Today, because of this, I'm at peace. I know that no one will lay a hand on me, no one will cross my boundaries. I realize there's more than just my family's awareness. I know life can be different. I found my dream place. Here, it doesn't matter how you live, or what you wear. No one competes with each other, no judgment, no harm. I always wanted to experience life in such a place.

A few years ago, before my second pregnancy, I went through a period where my mental state was screaming for help. I explained away my frequent panic attacks as being due to lack of sleep, poor diet, or anything else. Initially, I didn't realize that what was happening to me was connected to my mind and emerging memories. Fortunately, I slowly began to realize what I needed to do and started seeking help. This coincided with the time I met Artur, which was probably a significant influence.

One hundred kilometers from Hamburg, in Bremen, I found a place I could turn to. This woman was a therapist, a sexologist, and a couples co-unselor. I really liked her photo, so I chose her intuitively. During my first therapy session, I cried, shared my pain, and released my emotions. After that visit, I left her office tired but satisfied. After the second visit, the the-rapist suggested I should leave and immediately go or call my father to tell him everything. I told her that seemed like a bad idea. I added that I was simply afraid of him, hadn't worked through this fear, and confronting him was too big a challenge for me. Additionally, he had recently had a heart attack, and the shock could provoke another one. So, that was my second and last visit with her, after which I stopped therapy for about six months. During that time, I felt no therapist could help me, that they wouldn't be able to handle it, and why should I relive everything without any support? I thought I could handle it myself. But I couldn't.

A few weeks later, I found another therapist with an office close to me. I scheduled an appointment, but she canceled the day before. I should have taken that as a sign, as therapists rarely postpone sessions knowing how important these appointments are for their clients. The second sign was when I was supposed to go to the office, and she didn't give me the ad-dress. Eventually, I found it on her website, but it turned out to be her pri-vate home. Her husband answered the door and directed me to the office. I got lost and was frustrated with the situation, arriving about twenty mi-nutes late. I was annoyed at having arranged a session with a therapist who couldn't properly indicate the meeting place. No sign, proper address, or clear direction. But I finally got there. The place turned out to be more of a complex with various offices. We had forty minutes left for our session. For the first half hour, I talked about my past, what hurt me, what I had worked through, and where I still needed help. At one point, the therapist suddenly said that I was doing great. I'm a stripper, I earn good money, I'm brave, I travel, and I can take care of myself, so dwelling on the past is unnecessary. I should leave it behind and move forward, focusing only on the future. I responded okay, but I couldn't move forward with all this baggage; it was too heavy. I find it funny now, but then I started explaining to her why I needed therapy. She didn't understand, so I gave up on her. Once again, I felt like few could handle it all, and perhaps that's why I ended up finding a third therapist.

I became pregnant again, waited three months, and then arranged for online therapy. After a few sessions, I felt that the therapist didn't fully understand my situation and wasn't as engaged in our meetings as she should have been. After our fourth meeting, she told me she couldn't help me, that it was too big for her to handle, and she simply didn't know how to guide me. She also refused to continue due to my pregnancy. At that point, I decided to wait again and only returned to seeking support after giving birth.

My last, fourth attempt at finding a therapist came when I realized that for about a month, I had been wallowing in misery every morning. I kept telling myself that I was insufficient, that I hadn't cleaned the house, the bistro, the terrace properly. That I was an inadequate mother, and that everything that happened in my childhood was my fault. This made me wake up every morning with swollen eyes, aching, and filled with a sick determination to do everything myself. I wanted to prove to the world that I could manage everything on my own. One day, I woke up in a particularly bad state. I went to the shower and vomited from stress. There was a moment when I sat in front of the computer and intuitively chose the best therapist for myself. I knew I was doing this for me and that I would have these sessions online, so it was the most comfortable for me.

The meeting with the fourth therapist was as usual. In the second session, I opened up more, but it was only in the third session that I started to trust her to some extent. I felt like a frightened child and it was hard for me to share everything with another person, not knowing if she would believe me. But I ended up with someone who conducted the sessions smoothly, not interfering with my outpourings. She didn't judge me, didn't ask irritating questions. She was there and supported me, conducting the meetings in the way I needed. She respected my pace, didn't rush me, and didn't give advice. I then felt that I had finally found the right therapist and started to engage in what she was sharing. I took her advice, learned to breathe calmly, and visualized my safe place, which was supposed to help me separate from stressful situations and memories. The therapy worked, but it was just the beginning of the journey.

One day, I had another panic attack and in a very bad state, I went to my family doctor. He prescribed strong medication but at the same time told me not to take them. Perhaps the mere fact that I had access to them was meant to calm me. Anyway, he explained that they were very strong, and highly addictive, and if I took one, I would likely sleep for the next several hours. He also reassured me that people with panic attacks often feel very safe just knowing they have the medication at hand. He was right, as indeed the mere thought of having the means to alleviate these attacks somewhat calmed me down.

I remember the heightened social phobia and fear of approaching customers in the bistro. I was afraid to approach strangers and be judged. I knew it was my overinterpretation, and that an unpleasant customer might occur maybe once in a hundred, once in two hundred guests. But at that time, my reason was asleep, and irrational fear was rampant.

Often, outsiders can't understand the behaviors of people with problems. Behavioral disorders are not something you can just control. A person struggling with a panic attack, or an irrational fear of a specific activity is lost, and a clear assessment of the situation is impossible for them. They can't "pull themselves together". They can't "calm down". They can't "think rationally". They can't brace themselves, snap out of it, and live normally. THEY CAN'T. If it were that simple, damn it! The worst part, however, is that a person grappling with their past, with depression, with a sense of helplessness, and all-consuming pain, along with the awareness that they are worthless, has to start wanting to live. Exactly. If they don't want to, if it doesn't click in their head that it's worth trying, then nothing will have greater value for them. Sometimes these people convince them-

selves that they live only for their children, their partners, or someone. But at the same time, they think and say that they don't even deserve the last scraps of love, support, and simply life. Sometimes the turning point is an accident, hitting rock bottom, or a very painful event. Sometimes it's a subtle sign from the environment. Sometimes it's the patience of loved ones.

During therapy, I felt resistance, I had to relive everything again, but I allowed myself to go through it all and felt that this was my only right path. I had meetings once a week. After each one, I had a task to do. I performed the tasks assigned by the therapist and eagerly awaited the moment when I could take the next step.

From the beginning, I told her that I wanted to write a book, work as a coach, and support other women. She then responded that yes, I could do it, because I had already done and lived through so much in my life, that it was natural and very much accessible for me. Then I replied that I wanted to do it, but I felt that I couldn't and shouldn't. Then she explained to me that I certainly could and provided arguments for such action. Such conversations lasted several meetings, during which she instilled in me the awareness that I really could. That I was worthy, that I would manage, and I could do everything I had dreamed of.

It was always hardest for me when discussing abuse. I felt it all in my body, my psyche, in my memories. Different situations would bring these memories back at the most unexpected moments. I couldn't take a normal shower, I couldn't lie down curling my legs under me, I couldn't have sex freely with my partner because suddenly images I didn't want to see could appear in my head.

For the first two or three months of therapy, as I talked about my past and worked on every aspect of it, I was constantly tense. I felt that my body didn't relax for even a moment. Most of the time, I clenched my jaws and fists. I smoked about forty cigarettes a day and ate very little. For several days at a stretch, I could eat just one meal a day and feel hungry, but not strong enough to distract me from my thoughts and stresses. So, I ignored it. I also felt guilty and regretful about spending money on therapy. I felt bad with every payment for a session with my therapist, even though I knew it was the right thing to do. It was uncomfortable to think that I was doing this for myself. I started to examine every situation and thought related to expenses, including those for myself. I remembered how any medical expense in my childhood would create a kind of hell at home. My parents always had a problem with it. So, I knew that my current emotions about spending were a result of my past, something I had to fight against. It took me about three months to explain all this to myself. It was only then that I discarded the thoughts that I was selfish and didn't deserve this therapy. I started to move out of the victim mentality and began to let go of those emotions of my younger self. I started working with my inner child, which I wrote about more in the next chapter.

I realized that every day I was fighting absurd paradoxes. On one hand, I knew the therapy wasn't very expensive, but on the other hand, it felt like too much because it was spent on me, and I probably didn't need it, inventing needs that had no connection to reality. So, even though I wasn't spending a fortune on treatment, I still berated myself that I could have spent that money differently, better, on someone else. This was not just with therapy, but with buying even the smallest thing for myself. Going to the hairdresser, buying a dress and cosmetics. It took a long time to convince myself that this belief, where I see myself as a less important person, comes from childhood. That's when I was taught that a woman in the house takes care of everyone around her, and only looks after herself if there's enough time and money. Even though I had done various things for myself before, it was always accompanied by a feeling of guilt. At some point, however, when I let go of that, I realized that other people's beliefs about this are unimportant and that I am just as valuable as anyone else.

Like my loved ones and everyone around me, and that I can spend the money I earn on myself. That I don't have to buy more clothes, toys, and games for each child every month. When that happened, spending money on myself became a pleasure and, even when going for a manicure, I stopped tensing my hands. This difference, the changed mood, and the approach made even my beautician feel better in my company. Even though there's a small language barrier between us, we felt good during such visits.

The first two months of therapy were the hardest for me. There were times when I stopped talking to anyone. When the memories came back and I had to confront them, reliving it all, I would shut myself away for days. Conversations about the first abuse, the first beating by my father, and the ignorance of my mother made all the feelings associated with them return, not allowing rational thoughts that came with therapy to take hold. It usually looked very similar. On Tuesday at eleven, I would finish my session with the therapist, and then until Thursday or even Friday, I wouldn't speak to anyone. Not even to my sons. I would respond to them in one short word, specifically and quickly. All of this was damn hard for me and I'm very glad I survived it. I began to practice becoming a healthy adult for myself, but at the same time, I started hearing different voices in my head telling me not to do it, that it was too much, and that I would make a fool of myself.

During the course of therapy, I tried to take care of myself through many constructive activities. I wrote in a journal, meditated, practiced yoga, ice bathing, and being in silence. Quieting down during walks in the forest made me stop fearing silence and the thoughts that came with it. After a few weeks, I noticed that both strangers and acquaintances, women with their problems, started coming to me. They wrote to me on Facebook, and Instagram, and sometimes came to the bistro. I felt I could help them. A woman with two children, whose partner was drinking, wrote to me; she didn't need practical advice but support and the belief that she would be able to handle her problem. About a week after our conversation, she called me to say she had found an apartment and moved out from her partner. She said she was the happiest person on Earth. The realization that I could inspire other women to change was very uplifting for me.

Working with the Inner Child

If you don't heal the child within you, don't take care of its emotions, and keep drowning out that inner cry for help, you won't heal and move forward. The inner child is not just the tucked-away emotions from childhood that directly and indirectly affect what you do and how you react to various situations in your life. Working to release these emotions allows you to reach your true self. It allows you to become a real, healthy adult.

Working with the Inner Child, in my opinion, is the first and most important step in healing oneself. For those with major childhood traumas, it is work that never ends. Like a task for a lifetime. This is also the case for me. From being unloved, not taken seriously, neglected, abused, beaten, and humiliated by the closest people. Working with the Inner Child is learning how to be supportive of yourself. It starts with noticing emotions, and observing your body's reactions in different situations. It is a beautiful work, bringing incredible effects of positive change in everyday functioning. It is also extremely difficult. Feeling anger, regret, and helplessness, which you felt as a defenseless child and observing how these moments affect our adult life.

The Inner Wounded Child lives in us as long as we don't allow our feelings to be heard. No external factors, such as relationships, alcohol, other substances, money, or career, can heal this. Self-love is the cure for many life's difficulties. However, not everyone, like me, is given the right to it in childhood. When you bestow upon yourself unconditional love, your relationship with yourself reaches a new level. You can work with the Inner Child in therapy, during meditation, hypnosis, writing in a journal, or writing a letter to your Inner Child. Through working with the Inner Child, we can learn to be a Healthy Adult for ourselves and become the best Mom and Dad for ourselves, especially if those figures in our lives let us down.

Maybe it's worth thinking of oneself as someone who deserves the best.

Perhaps it's time to take a childhood photo, look at that little child, and ask ourselves if we really should take care of ourselves last. After all, that child needs love, affection, closeness, food, sleep, rest, joy, and fulfillment. If we don't provide these things, it will always feel alone. Do we want to treat our Inner Child that way? Do you want to treat yourself that way?

Radical Forgiveness

There are ways to let go of a heavy past that I had no idea about. Perhaps not all of them would have worked for me, but I was lucky to find one that moved me to a completely new level of consciousness. The feeling of light-ness, deep breathing, and freedom is something invaluable.

It was only after the session of radical forgiveness, or rather about a few months after it, that I began to regain peace. Everything started coming out of me. I gradually forgave Helena, the entire extended family, and all the people who had hurt me in life. My father, brother, and mother. And myself. I realized that I wasn't an angel either and that I had also hurt many people in my life. I began to come out of the victim role and take care of myself. I felt that what I was doing for myself was simply my due. Then I noticed that people looked at me differently.

It was easier for me to live in my world and feel that I was a victim, that people had hurt and were hurting me, and that I was so poor. The hardest thing for me was to think that it all happened for a reason. Because it's hard to extract something good from such memories. What good can come out of the fact that my father drank?

During my development, I realized how unhappy Helena was. And when she saw that I didn't want to live according to her toxic beliefs, she couldn't stand me. She had a lot of bad beliefs and energy to work through, but she didn't do it, and all she could do was react to me with aggression. I was proof that one could live differently. That was a big discovery for me.

My father was her son. He was neglected and unloved, and didn't receive the affection a child should. Only when I understood this did I feel how sorry I was for them, that they couldn't just live well. Their behavior was steeped in twisted beliefs, a sense of lack, and guilt that piled up every day, not allowing them to breathe normally.

Today, I understand that I am a healer. Black sheep appear in families for a reason. I don't always agree to carry the burden I must, but there are more moments when I'm happy about it. I'm glad I'm a different woman than my mother, or my grandmothers and aunts. I don't necessarily like comparing myself to them, but sometimes, when I need it, I remind myself that only I invested in myself. Time and love. Only I learned languages, only I traveled, and only I worked on myself. Sometimes it scares me how much I still have to work through, but I already know that I don't have to prove anything to anyone. I don't need to elevate myself over others and tell others about my successes. I need to know and feel it for myself. I have to be proud of myself, and admiration in other people's eyes is completely unnecessary to me. I won the life for myself, not for others.

What does the process of radical forgiveness involve?

It starts with the realization that we forgive someone only for ourselves. Living with the resentment that Damian did something to me, that I wanted to take revenge on him, was very destructive for me. The purpose of radical forgiveness is to shed those negative burdens and move on with life. For me, it began around August last year, and effectively ended about eight months later. Several years of flashbacks, panic attacks, and fears that didn't let me function normally. In the end, I felt very sorry for Damian and realized that I had to experience all this so I could work with women who had similar experiences. I also stopped looking at these events from a victim's perspective. Writing and recording about my childhood, I had to re-enter those negative emotions because I had practically forgiven those people by then.

From a logical point of view, all my close ones should be in prison. My father for violence, my mother for ignorance, my brother for sexual abuse, and Helena for not providing normal living conditions for her children and for raising them in aggression toward others. Would they then understand what they lived and how they lived?

The process of radical forgiveness is a few meetings with an experienced person and a process consisting of several steps that need to be taken in order. It starts with realizing that forgiveness is the best option for us. Then you write a letter to the perpetrator.

I remember writing one or two sentences and tearing them to pieces. Then I wrote words of greeting and tore them up again because how can you greet your perpetrator? I took a clean sheet of paper and ran away from home. However, the second meeting was approaching, and I had to do it. And yet, I couldn't arouse anger in myself. I couldn't put myself in the victim's role anymore. I couldn't write in the letter that I wanted to hurt the perpetrator.

The next step is to read this letter and burn it. I did this by the river. The next stage is to imagine the person we want to forgive sitting opposite us and tell them what they did to us and how much it hurt. This was the hardest for me. Then we say how hard it is for us to forgive and how important it is for us. The next stage of the speech includes expressing the emotions we currently have toward that person. I remember that, contrary to myself and to my surprise, I felt concern for Damian. I was angry with him for not taking care of himself, for being homeless, and for how he directed his life.

Completing this sheet, I had to write at the end that I forgive. And then I had to read it aloud and felt very uncomfortable with it. I didn't like it, I couldn't understand how one could forgive such things. However, in the end, after the whole process, it is obvious to me, and the luxury of peace is something incredibly valuable to me.

The inventor of the method of radical forgiveness talks about how in the spiritual world, which the soul visits between incarnations, we meet other souls and analyze our lives on Earth. Later, each soul chooses an incarnation and gets, or chooses for itself, tasks to work through. I don't know if I believe that, but it's easier for me to accept this version than to think that people around me were just evil. This is my mission, and I can come out with it and help people, women who went through the same as me.

By radically forgiving and living in love for the perpetrator, you see more colors, taste your life more, and gain a peace you've never been able to feel before.

Helena from the Perspective of a Healthier Me

Returning to the past to examine my feelings is part of the therapy and self-healing process. The perspective of a child is just one of many that I have experienced. After the process of radical forgiveness, my view of many things and people underwent a complete transformation. The road to this was long and winding, but I made it. It turned out that I didn't have to feel regret, anger, and sadness toward others. Because it was only a burden for me.

It took me several years to understand Helena and that she lived a life she didn't want. She wanted to live in the city, be somewhere other than where she was. Subconsciously, she saw me as a competition. I lived a completely different life than they did. I traveled, was honest, and didn't speak ill of others behind their backs. I had the courage that my family members lacked. I was able to shout out my truth, something she never could, and this aroused aggression toward me in her. From her level, she saw in me a child, and later a woman, who would be able to fulfill herself. She couldn't reach that point, and didn't know how to move toward her fulfillment. She lived in her world full of hatred and envy of everyone. Slowly I understood this and gradually let go of the beliefs that I took very seriously as a child.

I remember Helena from a time when in May, all the women in the village would go to the cross and pray there every day. One such day, she saw me with light makeup, which she greatly disapproved of. She screamed that I looked like a forty-year-old, that it was unacceptable. I remember thinking at that time that everyone should do what they want. But she clearly stated that children are there to live according to the rules imposed by elders. Both she and everyone around me stifled my arguments about wanting to achieve something in life.

Now looking back at all these situations with Helena, I simply feel sorry. I feel sorry for her. I'm not angry with her anymore, I just feel pity. Back then, I reacted as best I could. I ran away, laughed at her, and talked back. Even then, subconsciously, I felt that she was taking her frustrations out on me. If she were still alive, I'd buy her flowers, hug her, and tell her to try to be happy for a moment. Maybe I'd buy her a trip so she could fulfill her biggest dream of seeing part of the world. Maybe I'd take her to a beautician to feel better in her female skin. It would be different. When I completely let go of her and understood her story, I felt much better about myself. I don't mind that I've gained a little weight, that I look a bit worse some days. In the past, I only left the house in full makeup. Always dressed up, made up, done up completely. Eventually, though, I managed to be comfortable in my skin, to dress in a way that was more comfortable for me. I stopped over-preparing for going out and started leaving the house as myself. I understood that I was a healthier version of myself.

Pandemic

Staying with one's thoughts can be terrifying. However, sometimes it's the only option to get to know oneself. Are we able to definitively determine what we like, what we don't, what we want to achieve in life, and what kind of people we don't want in our surroundings? Sometimes it's only a crisis that brings out all these answers.

In March 2020, it started to look like we'd be stuck at home. That's when the idea came to my mind to completely give up alcohol. I had already significantly reduced it before, but I still allowed myself drinks every few weeks when the opportunity arose. Alcohol greatly changed consciousness, at least in my case. After about two weeks, I began to observe myself closely. My thoughts, emotions, and movements. With many of them, I couldn't fully come to terms. I saw in myself the behaviors of my mother, Helena, and my father. For example, the immense need for control. When, for instance, someone moved something that I had earlier placed in a specific place, I would get furious. I was angry and my reactions were completely disproportionate to the situation. Observing myself, I felt that I needed to go further, find a job, and most importantly, someone who could help me. It wasn't just because I had completely given up alcohol, although I could certainly say that I saw everything more clearly. I was my own biggest obstacle, constantly thinking badly of myself.

I started meditating. I went for walks with my dog, using this as a way to kill time while we had to stay at home. I also started writing down everything that was happening again. I even bought a laptop in installments to motivate myself to write. But damn, it just wouldn't come out right. Every attempt to write a book ended after a few days with body pain, reluctance, and vomiting. Another attempt ended in failure. However, I found the strength to talk about the abuse with Artur. I had been gathering courage for weeks. Whenever I lay down, sat down, or just was near him, I was preparing to tell him. It was supposed to be three words:

"Artur, I was molested."

That's all. Just that. But every time I opened my mouth to say them, I couldn't produce any sound. Finally, I couldn't bear it any longer and told him while crying. At first, I sobbed so much that he couldn't understand anything. It felt a bit better to share it with someone. The second person who found out was my sister Agata. We had a really good relationship then. She would come to me every Saturday, stay the night, and sometimes we cooked together the next day. I told her, emphasizing that our mother didn't believe me. She looked at me carefully and said that she believed me. That she knew our brother and was well aware that he was capable of something like that. Those words were very important to me. Both Artur and Agata unlocked a kind of encouragement in me that I began to give myself.

During meditation, I looked for a person who gave me a sense of security. I listed in my mind both those who hurt me and those who loved me. I crossed people off the list, thinking they were not the ones. Finally, after about thirty minutes, it dawned on me that only I can give everything to myself. I can give myself that sense of security and only I can create a boundary through which no further harm will break through.

The following months went like this: I worked unloading goods in a store. I wanted to have my own money. However, after some time, it became quite burdensome for me. At that moment, it was very necessary for me, but waking up at five in the morning to rush to a place where not only was I earning little money but also not fulfilling myself, was not what I wanted. The idea came to me that it was time to take care of myself in this regard, and the idea of nail styling courses came to my mind. I planned to work from home and do nails for my clients there. Reluctantly, I returned to working with women.

After some time, I noticed a common feature of all my clients. I treated each of them the same. I opened the door for them, invited them to sit down, and made something warm to drink. Then I sat opposite them and took their hands to see what needed to be done. After determining what we were doing and how, when I started working, each one began to confide in me. They started telling me about their problems, successes, and other things happening in their lives. It both exhausted and intrigued me. I observed myself and my feelings and wanted to know why I inspired such trust. This observation brought me a lot of good.

A woman who I can call a witch used to come to me. She laid Tarot cards and, from my point of view, lived as she wanted. I remember telling her that I envied her. That she wasn't afraid and had such a supportive environment. She then said something to me that I remember to this day and that guided me throughout the entire healing process. She said that when we start being ourselves and living what we believe in, people who have to leave, leave. Then we clear the field around us, and people who will support us come. Now I know all this, but back then, I was a bit scared. When I talked about this with friends, I felt they couldn't understand me. They looked at me like I was crazy when, for example, I told them that I checked the meaning of my dream in the morning. I began to understand that when we show our true selves, not everyone resonates with us. I noticed that my acquaintances no longer served me. When I lost contact with someone, I would unfriend them on Facebook, delete their phone number, and other traces that I might come across in my daily life. And when only a few people remained from a large circle of friends, with whom I felt safe and calm, I realized that all my life I had been wearing masks and was for others the person they needed. I adjusted myself to acquaintances, not fully realizing how much I was straining myself. In the community of dancers, one had to lie and always be on guard. No one could know too much about you. The girls always made things difficult for each other, and unhealed female energy made me feel sick. Fending off guys, fending off clients, or many other jealousy-, pain-, and rejection-inducing situations. Looking at the women in my family, I noticed my mother, who could never express herself and just show who she was. I looked at Helena, who, despite a huge sense of injustice, artificially showed everyone that she was happy. Or Anita, my mother's sister, who never dared to move out of her parents' house and live her way. Even being pregnant with her second child, she couldn't move out of a toxic home. None of these women were thus able to live their way.

My clients, who confided in me, must have sensed my tacit approval of their behavior. They felt safe with me.

At one point, I read a lot and eventually came across the book "It Didn't Start with You" by Mark Wolynn. The first time I read it, I didn't quite grasp everything I should have. The second time, however, I understood much more and saw in my example that all the women in my family were unhappy. They had traumas, limitations, and lives they didn't want. I too had inherited many negative traits from them. Complaining, negative attitude, the belief in perpetual lack of money, or compulsive buying of unnecessary things. I remember going to a store in Krakow and looking at leather jackets and furs. At one point, I tried on a jacket and without much thought went to the cashier and said I would take it. When the cashier said the jacket cost four thousand zlotys, I was stunned, but I was so embarrassed that I said okay and paid. I wasn't able to say that the jacket was out of my budget. It was only when I got home that I realized what I had done. I couldn't say no and live the way I needed to. I wrote down all similar situations on paper and saw how much it all resembled both Helena and my father. Helena in the sense that she always had a problem with spending money, paying bills, and buying anything. And my father in that he always wanted to show that he had a lot of money. I remember when he returned from Germany, he would hide a thick wad of banknotes in his chest pocket and walk around the village bragging about how rich he was.

That wasn't me. I liked going to thrift stores because I could dress cheaply, colorfully, and originally there. I began to notice that I was living with beliefs that were not my own. So, I began analyzing my past, which helped me start seeing myself, my beliefs, needs, and traits. Women who came to me for nails told me about really intimate, terrible things. About rapes, aggression, and alcohol in the family. On the other hand, there were also women with an entirely different energy. They showed me that it's worth pursuing your own goals and living according to your ideals. Both these energies reinforced in me the belief that above all, I must take care of myself, stop reacting to opinions, and move forward, fulfilling my inner desires. I had to start accepting every part of myself and stop lowering my self-esteem. I was my own biggest critic, and I was the one standing in the way of my complete happiness. Others' words, behaviors, and actions were a reflection of themselves and should not affect me. When someone demeaned me, they were demeaning themselves. It was different, however, when I spoke badly of myself. I couldn't do that anymore and took away my permission to do so.

Learning all this took almost my entire pregnancy. And it wasn't until 2022 that I felt it was time to act, to look for someone to write this book with me. To finally share my story with people.

I often noticed that people I talked to either didn't see or hear me. This irritated and hurt me. I took it like the small, ignored girl I was, without considering that maybe it was worth simply repeating. In my childhood, my parents did the same. They didn't respond to my feelings, but from the perspective of time, I see that they didn't know how to do it. My mother couldn't handle the fact that I was colorful and so different from her. She cut my hair short, mocked my small breasts, and treated me condescendingly. There was no mother-daughter relationship, just a hurtful relationship between women. She competed with me from the beginning, which is and was incomprehensible. Sometimes I wonder what would come out of psychiatric studies of women from my life environment.

When I realized that understanding me was a challenge for them, life got a bit easier. Of course, it's not super easy and wonderful, especially since all these things, memories, and traumas come back to me. I often started to fear women again, afraid that they would start talking to me and behaving like the women from my childhood. I had to let go of that, work through it, and move on so as not to become like my mother or Helena. Even looking at my sister, who grew up without my father and whom I essentially didn't know in adult life, I can't say that it was much easier for her.

I think the pandemic opened the eyes of many people. They couldn't leave their homes and in many cases were left alone with their thoughts. Many of them started working on themselves. They had time to reflect on themselves, and work on their lives. And make a step in the right direction. I went through my most significant, most intense transformation during this period. It gave me a lot, and although I had always dabbled in spiritual development throughout my life, it was during the forced stay-at-home that I found my way to myself.

The Idea for the Book

The initial idea to write a book came to me several years ago, back when I was a dancer. I tried to write everything down by hand on paper, but each time I ended up tearing everything to pieces because I imagined it was pointless, that no one would read it, and that I would make a fool of myself.

During therapy, I started to realize that this was not right. I understood that the voices in my head were not mine and that these were not my beliefs. And the feeling that I couldn't talk about my past because I would hurt Helena, my father, and the rest of my family began to slowly disappear. I realized that I wasn't sharing this out of a desire for revenge, but because of a need to regain balance and perhaps to help someone in the future by adding faith and courage to their life. To explain that we don't have to follow the crowd and if mom and dad don't believe in us, it doesn't mean the world doesn't believe in us. The world is quite different.

As I began to practice changing beliefs, interesting people started to appear in my life. A man who visits our bistro writes books. He comes to the village from time to time and every morning, for a few hours, he goes to the forest and writes. At one point, I thought, why couldn't I do the same?

I tried a few times and started jotting down memories on paper. Everything started coming back, and when I finished work, I felt tension throughout my body. Dizziness and paralysis appeared, preventing me from taking a normal breath. I let it go one day, then the next, and finally, I realized I had to do it differently. A few days later, I came across information online that made me realize I could record all these memories. In an interview I read, there was mention of a book that was written from recordings. I figured that since I talk about all this in therapy and often talk to myself, this was the best option for me.

The Power of Visualization

When I was living in Hamburg, still in 2022, around January, I intensely visualized my new place of residence. I wanted to be in a calm place, away from rainy, crowded Hamburg. During meditation, I envisioned a place free of a heavy atmosphere, where I wouldn't be burdened with huge expenses. Suddenly, miracles started happening. Together with Artur, we went to visit his friends who lived outside the city, and it turned out that the kind of village I dreamed of existed. During a conversation, we mentioned that we wanted to move to a place in Austria, somewhere close to nature.

About two weeks later, we received a phone call that a fully equipped place was available for rent in that very area. The owners wanted to rent it out with everything included for a really small deposit. We were to have at our disposal furniture, appliances, and even cutlery. We could pack up and move right away. I couldn't believe it.

I dreamed of a place near a river, old buildings, and castles, which I had a weakness for. I wanted to live in a place with soul and history that would give me peace every day. I wanted to be surrounded by friendly, valuable faces and feel the harmony inside, which I desperately longed for. I had all this in my head already. I had seen it all, but when it appeared in my life, I just couldn't grasp it with my thoughts. The realization of my dreams was incredible, only reinforcing my belief that I was on the right path and everything I was beginning to feel was finally as it should be.

When we got the news about the place and learned that we had to drive six hundred kilometers to finalize everything, we didn't hesitate. Artur took time off, we packed up and drove. Even during the journey, I felt that this was it.

It happened just as I thought. Upon arrival, we stopped at Artur's friends' place and quickly had a talk with the owners of the property. Everything went smoothly, and within a few hours, we received a positive response from the owners. We had to sort it out quickly to know what to do next. Organizing the move had to start right away, as we had a lot of paperwork to do, not only with the move but also in relation to starting a business and beginning our new life.

It was the start of an adventure that I was excited about. I was on maternity leave and I remember my father strongly advised against it. He said I didn't know anything about it, that it was too risky, and that I should stay in Hamburg. But nothing was holding me in that city. In three months, I had to look for a job. And was I supposed to continue living in constant rush, depression, and sadness? Should I not exaggerate and keep living as he thought? He told me all this from his point of view. He wouldn't have done it. But I was never him, even if I could behave according to the patterns he ingrained in me for a long time.

It is said that life will give you everything you want. Not exactly. You have in life what you are, not what you want. If you think that you don't deserve love, money, and happiness, you will continue to feel empty and unhappy. But these feelings and beliefs are so strong that it's hard to change them overnight. Changing your mindset can take years. It requires time, consistency, and determination, and fortunately, I found that in myself.

I told my dad about wanting to lead women's circles. He criticized and ridiculed me, and when I asked why he thought I wasn't cut out for it, he couldn't answer. I said that I wanted to work in something that brings me joy and fulfillment, not something that kills my zest for life. He replied that no one in our family had ever succeeded in doing something like that and it was unlikely I would either. I tried to explain to him that Helena had died a long time ago and it was high time he stopped believing in the nonsense she had fed him. But these conversations no longer influenced what I intended to do. With Artur's help, I opened a business and we moved to our place on Earth.

On the first day, on the terrace of our bistro, I found flowers with a note of encouragement. The neighbors wished us luck and kept their fingers crossed for us to stay as long as possible. Other neighbors brought us chocolates and equally supportive notes. Everyone around was happy about our arrival, and gave us lots of ideas for expanding and developing the bistro. We were told what was missing and what was nearby. We got help writing the menu. We got help in everything. I was surrounded by many kind, wonderful people. When Artur cooked dishes from the new menu, the owners came to us with a group of twenty people to try everything and tell us if it was right. So, from the very first moment, we received energy that strongly drove us to act in this new area for us.

Working at the bistro from the beginning brought us great joy, especially since we had plenty of customers from the opening. The great pride and happiness that I could handle all this gave me immense satisfaction. It was a test that I passed with flying colors in my eyes. Driving there, I knew this was it, but somewhere in the back of my mind, I still believed I couldn't handle it. Driving to the place, we had neither a nanny for Jaromir nor a place in kindergarten. Rosa and her husband, who had worked with us for a few weeks, traveled with us. Eventually, they returned to Brazil, where they lived, and suddenly I was alone. I had to manage, and I did. I received a lot of compliments, and generally, every day, the environment and people built my worth. And I built it too.

After the whole season, I realized that I have the strength and power within me to live a happy life. I just need to live in the here and now, not in the past. Everything is important, but the first and most important thing is how I treat myself. That's when I decided to write a book. Initially, I didn't want to touch on the subject of childhood, but at the urging of my therapist, I began to write down my memories. Finally, on my thirty-third birthday, I decided that by my next birthday, the book would already be published. I would have it in my hand.

I knew then that my intuition was the most important thing. It suggested to me who I should be in contact with. I realized that I didn't have to keep people around me with whom I felt uncomfortable in any way. I started looking for solutions on how to deal with the panic attacks that I still experienced. I found them. I saw that when I let go of the voices of the past, which weren't mine, I could work wonders in my life. I felt that I loved myself and was proud of myself. That I did-

n't take the blame for what my brother and father did to me, that I had returned all that to them. And I forgave them. I no longer felt resentment toward them because I understand that what matters is what I feel about my life and actions, and that my happiness should be the most important to me. Of course, loved ones are important, but the fact is, if I am happy, my loved ones will be happy.

When I understood that my life was in my hands, I felt powerful. I felt that I could do everything I wanted. And I felt that I had chosen the best possible path for myself.

To the Reader

It is said that a person who has been hurt but feels a bond with their abuser has what is known as Stockholm syndrome. This means that despite the trauma to the soul and body, they still harbor feelings toward their tormentor that prompt them to feel tenderness, guilt, or a sense of responsibility, shame, and many other feelings that are inadequate for the situation. Unfortunately, this is not something one can get rid of just like that, and the process of emotional escape from the abuser is complicated and often prolonged.

During a conversation with Ania, who was transcribing the words in this book, I was asked how it is that I still keep in contact with my father. After everything he did to me? I thought about it and internally admitted that it was a mistake and that I should indeed stop calling him. I stopped for a few weeks, and eventually, he called me. He asked, out of forced politeness, how I was and then moved on to the topic of my sister. During the conversation, he activated a well-known pattern that methodically evoked in me an utterly unnecessary sense of guilt. He asked about my sister, and when I said I didn't know, he was displeased. I explained that Agata was depressed and perhaps harbored some resentment toward me which might be why she wasn't contacting me. Then he steered the conversation in such a way that I felt very bad. He suggested, and even stated outright, that it's my sister and it's my duty to do everything to help her. Even if she doesn't want it, it's my fault that she's not coping.

Another time, I felt I should call him and tell him that I was writing a book and that it would contain everything about my childhood and what he did to me. That I was writing my truth, as I saw it through my child's eyes, and I didn't care if he got offended. I felt bad about him, that I would hurt him with this and maybe I shouldn't do it. I imagined that he would indeed be offended and remind me of my feeling that I was lying. I know I am writing and telling the truth, but he has always convinced me that I'm not, that I'm lying and saying things that never happened. This feeling and this fear are as fucked up as they can be, and it makes me return to this sick state of confusion, and a part of me wants to believe that I am doing wrong. I know I'm moving forward, but getting out of this quagmire is harder than I thought.

I did an exercise where I entered several situations with my father. I put myself in a situation where I didn't tell my father about the book and then I felt great anger at myself for being a coward. Then I entered a situation where I told him and I felt immense guilt. Then I entered a third situation, where I told him at the right time for me, and I felt significantly lighter.

I went to my first therapy in my adult life, but I couldn't communicate with the therapist. Maybe I couldn't explain something to her, maybe there was no chemistry between us. After several years of searching, I finally found the right person for therapy and managed to complete it. Now I go to meetings every two weeks, which are a support for me, but I feel that this process is not yet finished.

When I read parts of the book to check if everything I wanted to convey was there, I re-enter those situations and become that little girl again. All this means that I go through this path again, and sometimes it's really hard for me. Attacks of fear and panic paralyze me to the extent that tasks that I previously performed easily become insurmountable. One day, I couldn't leave the bar in the bistro for two hours because I was afraid. My body was tense, and I couldn't catch my breath. I felt as if people around me were looking at me the way my family used to. It was terrifying. A traumatic, painful return to childhood with a full range of emotions that I experienced back then.

I remember the turmoil in Poland over the strict abortion law. I was in Germany at the time and couldn't participate in the protests. But I really wanted to. I was in the early stages of pregnancy and my emotional state was something new to me. I drove to the consulate in Hamburg with banners and was there with other women. I wanted to feel united with them. Watching the news and seeing the streets of Warsaw filled with women, I felt a desire to help them. It was the beginning of my certainty about what I wanted to do in life. I wanted to teach them that we can be together, work together, and be with other women without comparing ourselves, without jealousy, and without the difficult and negative emotions that disrupt our inner selves.

Recently, I had my first meeting, originally meant to have several women attend. In the end, only one came because the other three canceled shortly before the event. It was meant to be that way, and I still took a lesson from it. Together with the woman who visited, we gave each other everything we needed at the moment and I can confidently say it was very constructive.

I want to create a safe place for women in crises. For those affected by psychological or physical violence. Perhaps it will also be a haven for teenagers who want to escape from a home where they don't feel safe. I want to create a place where women can come back to themselves and feel that, over time, they will be able to give themselves what they need. A place where women feel special, that they don't need to prove anything to anyone. Where they don't have to worry about others' opinions, where they can set boundaries and are responsible only for themselves, not for what others do to them. Where they don't have to take the blame. Where they have strength and agency. Where they can achieve their dreams and feel happy and beautiful. Where they have the right to decide about their bodies and their future. Where they have the right to respect, to peace, silence, support, and to have bad moments. Where they can put themselves first and be independent and complete within themselves. I want Polish women to reclaim their power. And that is now my dream.

My most important message, which I want to resonate in this book, is that a bad chapter in your life does not define your future. It doesn't matter if it's about your childhood or mistakes in adult life. At any age, you can and have the right to start living with love and respect for yourself. What my parents, family, and others said to me and how they treated me was not about me. It was about them. They couldn't accept that I was DIFFE-RENT. That I had BIGGER dreams. That I FELT more. That I SAW the world differently. That I WANTED to live differently. They tried to change me in various ways. Over time, perhaps out of fear or helplessness, I began to resemble them. Then, when I got used to my difficult situation, I stopped seeing the magic and goodness of the world. When I regained my SELF, I decided that no one could ever hurt me again. And I forgave my childhood oppressors. By doing so, I stopped being a victim. I decided to work on my childhood traumas until I healed my bruised soul. That I would step by step fulfill my dreams. That I would shed the fears acquired in childhood so that I could finally embrace life fully. And the family I grew up in was just a tool to become a better version of myself. And I should not take them as an example and remember the life I don't want to live. For many years, I had a strong need to forget it all. But when that didn't work, I decided to turn it into something good. Empathy and high sensitivity are my great gifts. I want to use them to help others. I know what it's like to be a defenseless victim, waiting passively for a savior. I know how hard it is to clear your head of beliefs that aren't your own. How hard it is to believe in yourself. How hard it is to return to your power. And regain control over yourself. And agency. Because I managed to do it, I want others to believe they can too. This book is one of the tools I want to use to fulfill my dreams and help others on a larger scale.

It's a hard book, a hard life, a hard subject.

But very necessary.

Many women suppress similar experiences within themselves, and it never does them any good; others are currently going through similar things. I know that Ania's mission is just beginning, and after a tumultuous story where the reader experiences a range of negative emotions and probably judgments toward Ania and others, in the end, they were able to transition into positive feelings and understanding, as well as draw many personal conclusions. Ania showed a true story here and you can feel that she didn't care what others would think.

This story is so real and true that it awakens us from the illusion that such things don't happen around us, or to us. It teaches us that such shocking, painful experiences should not be a taboo subject, should not be hidden, and silence is consent for them to continue. It's a very educational story and I hope it will be liberating for many women, and will change the be-havior of many people.

221

Special thanks to:

My therapist, Adrianna:
Thanks to you, I regained courage and abandoned fear.
I thank myself:
For everything I have done for myself.

I thank Ania Gajowniczek:
For the work she put into this book.

9 788397 031838